W9-BEX-899

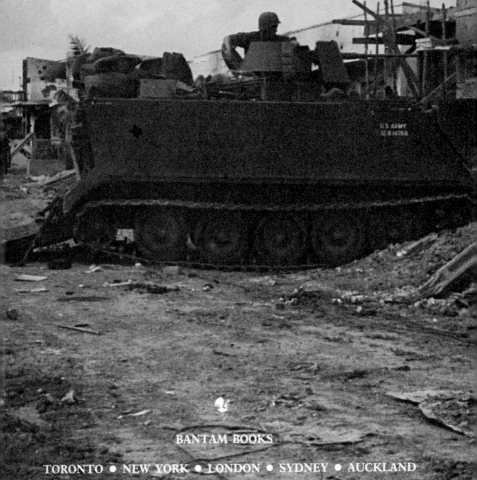

BANTAM BOOKS

TORONTO • NEW YORK • LONDON • SYDNEY • AUCKLAND

TET—1968

by
Jack Shulimson

THE BATTLE FOR SAIGON

The quick and the dead coexist on the streets of Saigon. Pedestrians walk unconcernedly past the body of a Viet Cong guerrilla on 31 January 1968, the morning after the enemy's night attack on the capital.

HOUSE-TO-HOUSE SEARCH

Airborne troops of the 2d Bn, 506th Infantry,
supported by tanks of the 11th Armored Cavalry,
search a hamlet for Viet Cong guerrillas who
staged a surprise attack on the US air base at
Binh Hoa during the Tet uprising. US forces
countered by sending mechanized
reinforcements from Long Binh to secure
Route 1 and contain enemy attacks.

JUST WAITING

During the heavy fighting for southern Hue, two Marines take shelter behind a partly demolished wall while waiting for fire support to soften up the enemy so they can storm the courtyard.

SNIPER BATTLE

During the fighting at Hue two Marine infantrymen from Co. A, 1st Bn, 1st Marines, use a vantage point in a deserted attic to try and locate and take out enemy snipers.

MOPPING UP

Men from Co L, 3d Bn, 5th Marines, on a search-and-destroy mission, move across a rice paddy between the coast and Hue after NVA troops had been spotted in the area.

EDITOR-IN-CHIEF: Ian Ballantine

SERIES EDITOR: Richard Grant.
SERIES ASSOCIATE: Richard Ballantine.
MAPS: Kim Williams.
PRODUCED BY: The Up & Coming Publishing Company, Bearsville, New York.

TET-1968
THE ILLUSTRATED HISTORY OF THE VIETNAM WAR
A Bantam Book/ December 1988

DEDICATION

*To my wife Corinne who is responsible for most of the good things in
my life.*

ACKNOWLEDGEMENTS

*I wish to thank Captain Alexander W. Wells, Jr., USMCR, for permission to
use and quote from his unpublished narrative on his own experiences in the
Citadel in Hue during Tet. I also wish to acknowledge my debt to Brigadier
General Edwin H. Simmons for his close reading of my manuscript.
However, I alone am responsible for opinions expressed and any factual
errors in the text. In no way do any of the opinions expressed in this book
represent the views of the US Government or the US Marine Corps.*

*Photographs for this book were selected from the archives of Camera Press,
the Defense Still Media Depository, MARS, and Popperfoto.*

All rights reserved
Copyright © 1988 Rufus Publications, Inc.
*No part of this book may be reproduced or transmitted in any form or by
any means, electronic or mechanical, including photocopying, recording, or
by any information storage and retrieval system, without permission in
writing from the publisher.*
For information address: Bantam Books

Library of Congress Cataloging-in-Publication Data
Shulimson, Jack.
Tet—1968.

(The Illustrated history of the Vietnam War)
1. Tet Offensive, 1968.   I. Title.   II. Series.
DS557.8.T4S58   1988   959.704'342   88-8143
ISBN 0–553–34582–6

Published simultaneously in the United States and Canada

*Bantam Books are published by Bantam Books, a division of Bantam Doubleday Dell
Publishing Group, Inc. Its trademark, consisting of the words "Bantam Books" and
the portrayal of a rooster, is Registered in U.S. Patent and Trademark Office and in
other countries. Marca Registrada. Bantam Books, 666 Fifth Avenue, New York, New
York 10103.*

PRINTED IN THE UNITED STATES OF AMERICA

CW 0   9   8   7   6   5   4   3   2   1

Contents

Attack on the Embassy

A FEW MINUTES after midnight on 31 January 1968, the first night of Tet, the Vietnamese Lunar New Year, a small commando group of less than 20 men from the C-10 Battalion of the Communist South Vietnam People's Liberation Army, more familiarly known as the Viet Cong or VC, assembled in a small auto repair shop, five blocks from the American Embassy compound in downtown Saigon. The soldiers broke out their weapons and listened to a hasty briefing on their mission. About 0230 hours, they piled into a Peugeot panel truck and an old taxicab and drove through the now largely empty Saigon streets.

At 0245 hours the two vehicles approached the intersection of Mac Dinh Chi Street and Thong Nhut Boulevard, the location of the formidable-looking walled compound encasing the six-story Embassy chancery and support buildings. They then made a left onto Thong Phut with the truck in the lead. As the taxicab rounded the corner, the men inside fired upon two US Military Police (MPs) manning the night gate. The Americans returned the fire, slammed the steel door of the gate shut, and radioed the codeword "Signal 300," sounding the alarm that the embassy was under attack.

Both the truck and cab came to a stop and the armed VC jumped out. With a 15-pound plastic charge, they blasted a large hole in the wall. The two American MPs, Specialist Fourth Class Charles L. Daniel and Private First Class William E. Sebast, turned around to face the invaders. Daniel yelled

Attack on the Embassy

SUICIDE ATTACK?
A Viet Cong commando lies dead in the courtyard of the American Embassy compound after taking part in a 6½-hour battle to take control of the Embassy. A B-40 antitank rocket launcher is to the left of his body. This attack on the seat of American power in Vietnam was symbolic; the VC had little hope of securing the Embassy when battalions of US troops were less than an hour away. But the attack had the desired effect, making front-page news in US newspapers the next day.

into his radio that the enemy was coming in. The Viet Cong killed both MPs. Two more MPs, Sergeant Jonie B. Thomas and Specialist Fourth Class Owen E. Mebust, died in a burst of Communist machine gun bullets, when they responded to Daniel's appeal.

For the next six and a half hours, US soldiers and Marines, reinforced by South Vietnamese police, battled with the Communist infiltrators within the American Embassy compound. At 0915 hours the next morning, the American command announced that the Embassy was secure. Five minutes later, US Army General William C. Westmoreland, Commander, United States Military Assistance Command, Vietnam, strode through the smashed gate of the compound. The bodies of the dead MPs and their VC assailants still lay strewn about the

courtyard. The US suffered casualties of six killed
and five wounded. Also among the dead were four
South Vietnamese civilian employees of the
Embassy. Four of the attackers from the VC C-10
Battalion had been killed and two taken prisoner.

In an impromptu press conference, Westmoreland,
dressed in starched and pressed fatigues, claimed
that the enemy's plan had been foiled and that
American and South Vietnamese units were now on
the offensive. Yet, millions of Americans saw on
their evening television news shows scenes of their
own embassy under siege. Although described as a
"piddling platoon action," the attack on the embassy
dominated American newspaper headlines and came
to symbolize the frustrations of a long and puzzling
war.

A nation at war

EXCEPT FOR A BRIEF RESPITE during the mid-1950s, Vietnam, as 1968 began, was a country that had been at war for over 20 years. The conflict had begun with the Communist-led insurgency against the French following World War II, eventually leading to the French defeat at Dien Bien Phu. This, in turn, led to the Geneva Accords in 1954 resulting in the division of Vietnam along the 17th Parallel. A 10-kilometer-wide demilitarized zone (DMZ) separated the two Vietnams. The Communist leader Ho Chi Minh in Hanoi proclaimed the Democratic Republic of Vietnam in the north and Ngo Dinh Diem, a strong anti-Communist Vietnamese nationalist, became the first president of the Republic of Vietnam in Saigon.

South Vietnam extended from the Ben Hai river in the north to the Cau Mau peninsula to the south, a distance of some 750 miles. The Annamite mountain chain dominated the terrain in the west and covered nearly two-thirds of the country. A spur of the Annamites nearly runs into the sea at the Hai Van Pass, isolating the northern two provinces of Quang Tri and Thua Thien from the rest of South Vietnam. In the center of the country, the mountains break down into the Central Highlands. Divided into 44 provinces, South Vietnam had a population of about 15 million people. Route 1 and a single gauge railroad that paralleled the long coastline were the main north-south lines of communication.

Through the late 1950s and into the 1960s, Diem consolidated his power in the South. By 1962, with South Vietnam facing a northern-inspired Communist insurrection, the United States established its Military Assistance Command Vietnam (MACV) to assist the Diem regime.

TURNING POINT:
A French paratrooper waits in a trench on the perimeter of the airfield at Dien Bien Phu in the spring of 1954. Within weeks the Communist Viet Minh would overrun the French position. It was a defeat that echoed round the world and led to the eventual division of the country into two Vietnams.

Despite American assistance, the Viet Cong guerrilla war against the southern government intensified. In securing his base of power in the South, President Diem, a Catholic, alienated large segments of the Buddhist establishment. In November 1963, the South Vietnamese military with the acquiescence of the US government overthrew Diem. With the coup, the situation in South Vietnam deteriorated. The Communist Viet Cong gathered strength and North Vietnamese units were identified in the South.

In the spring of 1965, the United States sent its first ground combat units to South Vietnam to stave off what appeared to be certain defeat. By January 1968, MACV numbered 486,000 US Marines, soldiers, sailors, and airmen. With the expansion of US forces, the Americans had taken over from the South Vietnamese much of the large-unit war against the Viet Cong main force and North Vietnamese regular battalions and regiments.

The US commander, General Westmoreland, had his tactical units grouped into three regional commands that roughly corresponded to the corps areas of the Republic of Vietnam. The III Marine Amphibious Force (III MAF) was deployed in I Corps, the five northern provinces of South Vietnam. The I Field Force, Vietnam, was in South Vietnam's II Corps, situated in the Central Highlands and the central coastal provinces. Further south, the II Field Force operated in both III Corps and northern IV Corps. Troops from Korea, Australia, New Zealand, and Thailand augmented the American combat forces.

Command arrangements, like the US commitment, evolved over time without any master plan. Westmoreland, who had presided over the buildup and commitment of US troops, had full responsibility for the conduct of the war in the South. He exercised his authority within an American chain of command that extended from Washington to Saigon. The American service components in South Vietnam both complicated and occasionally blurred the command arrangements within MACV. Complicating command lines even further were MACV relations with external US commands, the US Embassy in South Vietnam, and the South Vietnamese themselves.

The relationship with the South Vietnamese military was a delicate one. General Westmoreland did not have command of the South Vietnamese Armed Forces, and indeed, he rejected the idea of a combined American-South Vietnamese command headquarters. He believed that his role as senior US advisor to the South Vietnamese Joint General Staff gave him "defacto control" over the Vietnamese forces. The watchwords were close consultation and coordination.

By the end of 1967, the South Vietnamese Gov-

President Ngo Dinh Diem —South Vietnam's first president. He was installed in office after the Geneva Accords divided the country in two. A fierce anti-Communist, he quickly proved to be an unpopular dictator and eventually lost the American support he required to maintain power. He was murdered in a military coup in 1963.

ALLIED POWER:
Troops from the Republic of Korea (ROK) Tiger division fire a 4.2-inch mortar during an action in Binh Dinh province. In the early years of the US involvement, American and ARVN forces were supported by troops from Australia, New Zealand, Korea, and Thailand. The 50,000-strong all-volunteer ROK force gained a reputation for effective cordon-and-search operations—and scrounging supplies.

ernment had established a constitutional claim to legitimacy. In September 1967 South Vietnam elected the phlegmatic General Nguyen Van Thieu and the flamboyant Air Marshall Nguyen Cao Ky, heading a military slate of candidates, as President and Vice President, respectively, of the Republic of Vietnam.

As complex as the US and South Vietnamese command relations were, the Communist control apparatus to Western observers appeared even murkier. Yet, there was no question about who was in charge. From the beginning of the Viet Cong insurgency, the North Vietnamese directed the war, but masked their direct control through a web of cover organizations. The North Vietnamese went to extraordinary lengths to conceal their participation, even to the extent of changing the name of the party in the South from Workers Party to the People's Revolutionary Party.

In the South, the Communists created a Central

Office for South Vietnam (COSVN) to coordinate both the political and military aspects of the war. Under COSVN, a myriad of interlocking regional, provincial, and district committees tightly controlled the Viet Cong political infrastructure and military forces down to the hamlet and village level. Yet COSVN itself reported directly to the Politburo of the Lao Dong Party of North Vietnam through the Reunification Department with its headquarters in Hanoi. Despite denials and elaborate attempts by the North Vietnamese to cover troop movements through constantly changing unit designations, MACV in 1967 identified seven North Vietnamese Army Divisions within South Vietnam, five of these divisions in I and II Corps.

Nguyen Cao Ky —A flamboyant fighter pilot and Air Marshal in the Vietnamese Air Force, he served as president from 1965-67. In South Vietnam's first elections in September 1967 he ran on a military slate and was elected vice-president.

By the end of the year the American command held in its order of battle of enemy forces 216,000 troops. This included 51,000 North Vietnamese regulars, 60,000 Viet Cong main and local forces, and about 70,000 full-time guerrillas. Roughly 35,000 administrative troops rounded out the total.

The MACV estimate, however, omitted certain categories such as VC "self-defense" forces and other irregulars and some 70,000 political cadres. Although extensive disagreement existed within the US intelligence community over these exclusions and the total strength of the enemy, the numbers of regulars and full-time guerrillas were largely accepted. As General Westmoreland later explained, "Intelligence is at best an imprecise science—it is not like counting beans: it is more like estimating cockroaches. . . ." More open to question was the MACV claim that the total enemy strength had diminished.

From an American perspective, the Communists had suffered only defeats since the US intervention in the war in 1965. American units in extensive operations had taken a large toll of enemy forces. The allies turned back—with heavy losses—every thrust by the North Vietnamese Army (NVA) from the Ia Drang valley in the Central Highlands during 1965 to the hills surrounding the Marine base at Khe Sanh during the spring of 1967. For that year alone, MACV estimated the number of enemy killed in battle as over 88,000.

The Communist viewpoint still remains unknown. In the summer of 1967, the North

A nation at war

ANGEL OF CON THIEN: A CH-53A Sea Stallion of Marine Heavy Helicopter Squadron 463 airlifts supplies into the Marine outpost at Con Thien in the fall of 1967. The 158-meter high hilltop south of the DMZ came under a month-long attack during the NVA's 1967-68 Winter-Spring campaign. The attack was eventually broken with the aid of over 700 B-52 bomber strikes.

Vietnamese Defense Minister and the architect of Communist victory at Dien Bien Phu, Vo Nguyen Giap, claimed that the Communist forces were winning victory after victory: " . . . the situation has never been as favorable as it is now." Apparently, however, the North Vietnamese leadership had serious differences among themselves as to their best course of action. Some advocated a reversion to guerrilla warfare and a protracted war while others were proponents of renewed offensives against the allies and especially the Americans on all fronts.

Because of the extraordinary secretiveness and paranoia within the higher reaches of both the Lao Dong Party and the North Vietnamese government, neither the extent of these differences nor even the

makeup of the opposing factions was obvious. Much speculation centered around Giap, who at a June 1967 politburo meeting to resolve the issues, called for a "decisive blow" to force the US out of the war.

Within a few months the Communists launched the first phase of their 1967-68 Winter-Spring Campaign. Reversing their usual tactics, the North Vietnamese massed assaults lasting over a period of several days instead of disengaging. In September and October, North Vietnamese infantry and artillery struck at Con Thien, the Marine outpost in the eastern DMZ sector.

Repulsed at Con Thien, the Communists then turned south. On 27 October, the NVA 88th Regiment attacked the command post of the 3d

A nation at war

DAK TO AND HILL 875: Sky soldiers of the 173d Airborne Brigade clear a trench in preparation for an assault on the shell-battered slopes of Hill 875 during the battles around Dak To in November 1967. The 22-day long action near the Cambodian border climaxed in a long and bloody fight to oust an NVA regiment dug in on Hill 875.

Battalion, 9th ARVN Regiment near the village of Song Be in northern III Corps. The ARVN threw back the attackers with heavy losses. Two days later a Viet Cong Main Force regiment attempted to take the district capital of Loc Ninh near the Cambodian border north of Saigon. Allied forces forced the enemy to retreat with heavy losses in a running engagement that lasted for several days.

The heaviest fighting occurred in November in the Central Highlands near the hamlet of Dak To.

For 22 bloody days in November, units of the US 1st Cavalry Division (Airmobile), 4th Infantry Division, and 173d Airborne Brigade supported by 10 South Vietnamese battalions fought four North Vietnamese regiments in the surrounding rugged mountains. The North Vietnamese finally withdrew into their base areas in Laos and Cambodia, sustaining staggering casualties.

Despite the signs of an enemy buildup, General Westmoreland voiced his optimism about the course

President Lyndon B. Johnson —As 1967 closed he was publicly optimistic about the future of the war. But in private he warned the Australian cabinet of "dark days ahead."

of the war. Called back to Washington in mid-November 1967, ostensibly for consultation but more to shore up public support for the administration's Vietnam policy, he assured his audiences that the end was in view and that the "ranks of the Viet Cong are thinning steadily." Reflecting this same optimism in his directives, Westmoreland advised his subordinate commanders that the situation was "conducive to initiating an all-out offensive on all fronts—political, military, economic, and psychological."

With the coming of the Christmas and New Year holiday season, the war continued on its ambivalent course. The seasonal truce periods revealed certain cross-currents of the conflict. Giving vague hints of peace, the Communists agreed to a 24-hour truce over Christmas and a slightly longer 36-hour respite over New Year. Taking advantage of the cease-fire and the halt in American air operations, the North Vietnamese moved supplies to their forward units. During Christmas, US air observers spotted 600-800 vehicles and boats hauling and landing military provisions and equipment in southern North Vietnam. MACV reported 118 enemy violations over Christmas and 170 during the New Year's truce period.

The American command called both the Christmas and New Year's stand-downs a "hoax" and recommended that any cease-fire for the Vietnamese Tet or Lunar New Year be as short as possible. Although the American command would have preferred no Tet truce, President Thieu insisted that the Tet holiday was too important for the Vietnamese people to cancel a truce altogether. Westmoreland, nevertheless, persuaded the South Vietnamese leadership to shorten the truce period to 36 hours.

US leaders worried over the Communist intentions for the new year. In a departure from the optimistic public rhetoric of his administration about the war, President Johnson warned the Australian cabinet in late December of "dark days ahead."

Much evidence indicated that the enemy was on the move. Captured enemy documents spoke of major offensives throughout South Vietnam. One in particular observed "that the opportunity for a general offensive and general uprising is within reach. . . ." and directed the coordination of military attacks "with the uprisings of the local population to take over towns and cities."

By January 1968, a sense of foreboding and uncertainty dominated much American thinking about the situation in Vietnam and the way the war was progressing. According to all allied reports, Communist forces had taken horrendous casualties during the past few months, causing one senior US Army general to wonder if the North Vietnamese military command was aware of these losses. Yet, all the signs pointed to a major enemy offensive in the very near future.

Lieutenant General Frederick C. Weyand, the commander of the II Field Force, a lanky serious man and former intelligence officer, was convinced that Viet Cong forces were moving out of their border sanctuaries towards populated areas including Saigon. He met with General Westmoreland on 10 January and asked the MACV commander to postpone an operation in Phouc Long province near the Cambodian border. Convinced by Weyand's arguments, Westmoreland agreed to pull back the American forces to cover the Vietnamese capital.

Despite his precautions in III Corps, Westmoreland's attention remained focused on I Corps. With mounting evidence of an enemy offensive at Khe Sanh, the allied command revoked the truce in the northern two provinces. To Westmoreland and his staff, the Communist strategy appeared clear. The North Vietnamese wanted to draw the allied forces into remote areas, especially in northern I Corps, where the enemy had the advantage of terrain and shorter supply lines, and then move to a "mobile War of Decision."

Lt. Gen. Fred C. Weyand —The commander of II Field Force. By early January 1968 he was convinced that the Viet Cong were planning a major offensive.When it came, enemy rockets ripped apart his command headquarters at Loc Binh.

Looking north

The Marines and MACV

I CORPS dominated Westmoreland's thinking more and more. Consisting of the five northern provinces of South Vietnam, I Corps was known in MACV circles as "Marine land" because the III Marine Amphibious Force, since 1965, had controlled all American operations in the region. With its headquarters at the sprawling and centrally located Da Nang base, III MAF in January 1968 numbered over 100,000 Marines, sailors, and soldiers, nearly a quarter of the total American strength in South Vietnam. Its 53-year-old commander, Lieutenant General Robert E. Cushman, commanded nearly a field army in size. Despite its apparent strength, III MAF was spread thin to cover the 220 miles extending from the DMZ in the north to the border of II Corps in the south.

After the incursion of North Vietnamese regulars through the DMZ in the summer of 1966, the 3d Marine Division was moved north to meet the challenge. Forced to fill the gap in southern I Corps, MACV, in 1967, reinforced the Marines with the US Army units that formed the 23d Americal Division. This northward deployment resulted in the DMZ sector and Khe Sanh becoming the focus of allied concern.

Given this emphasis on the northern battlefield, General Westmoreland in April 1967 directed the Marines to erect a strong point obstacle system along the DMZ to prevent North Vietnamese infiltration. Unceremoniously labeled the "McNamara Line" by reporters after the US Secretary of Defense Robert S. McNamara, this so-called "barrier" was to consist of a linear manned obstacle system in the eastern DMZ followed by a series of strong points with Khe Sanh as its western

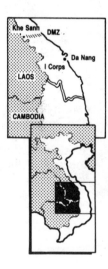

anchor. Acoustical and seismic sensors were to be deployed to pick up sounds and movements.

The "McNamara line" remained a constant irritant between MACV and III MAF. General Cushman recalled that Army engineer colonels from MACV "would come roaring up from Saigon to see how the fence was doing and . . . I'd say 'well it's doing fine, go up and take a look,' which they did." Cushman remarked that MACV "always had a few people around, but we just weren't going out getting everybody killed building that stupid fence."

Major General Rathvon McC Tompkins, the soft-spoken but blunt commander of the 3d Marine Division, voiced the opinion of most Marines when he later called the entire barrier effort "absurd." He pointed out that the original design was to stop infiltration, but by the time actual construction began, the North Vietnamese were in strength in the DMZ "supported by first class artillery." Tompkins caustically observed, "it was perfectly obvious that if there would be an incursion, it would be by NVA divisions and not by sneaky-peekies coming through at night."

Maj. Gen. Rathvon McC Tompkins —As commander of the 3d Marine Division, he considered the concept of the McNamara Line "absurd."

While reinforcing the Marines in I Corps with Army units and concentrating his forces in the north, Westmoreland had growing doubts about the ability of the Marine command to handle the developing situation.

From the Marine viewpoint more emphasis needed to be placed on the pacification effort and the small-unit war in the villages to protect the people. General Westmoreland and his staff, on the other hand, perceived the principal mission of the US troops to be the defeat of the enemy main forces.

The dispute over priorities never came to an actual head. Rather than directly challenge the authority of the Marine commanders, General Westmoreland preferred to issue "orders for specific projects . . . (to) get the Marines out of their beachheads." Lieutenant General Cushman, the III MAF commander, also wanted no controversy: "I soon figured out how Westy (General Westmoreland) liked to operate and tried to operate the same way, and get on with the war and not cause a lot of friction for no good reason."

In spite of the efforts of both Westmoreland and Cushman to keep their relationship on an even keel,

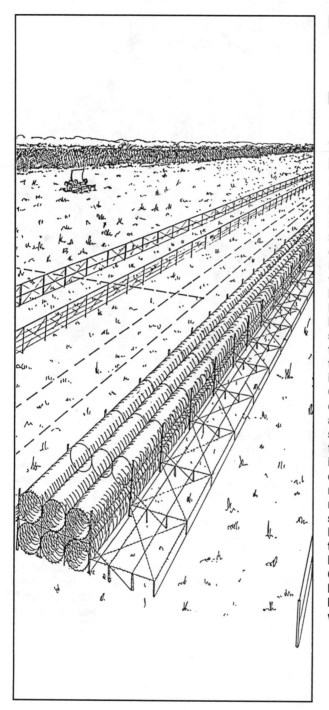

Looking north

THE MCNAMARA LINE:

Named after Robert S. McNamara, the Defense Secretary who endorsed it, the McNamara Line was intended to be a 160-mile long physical barrier stretching from the sea along the DMZ and into Laos. Consisting of an electrified fence and a matrix of sensors, the fence was intended to detect the movement of men and supplies heading south through the DMZ. Only a few kilometers were built before it was abandoned.

COMMANDING STYLES:
Differences in priorities and style marked the relationship between the overall US commander, Gen. William C. Westmoreland (left) and Lt. Gen. Robert E. Cushman, the III MAF commander (right). Cushman placed more emphasis on pacification and the small-unit war in the villages. Westmoreland perceived the principal mission was to defeat the enemy main forces.

substantive differences between the two continued to exist.

The differing personalities and styles of Generals Westmoreland and Cushman also tempered MACV-III MAF command relations. A large bulky man, the bespectacled Cushman offered a sharp contrast to the rigid military bearing of Westmoreland, who appeared to be "standing at attention while on the tennis court." The MACV commander insisted on detailed plans of operations with no loose ends. By contrast, General Cushman maintained an informal structure, confiding in few, and relying heavily on his chief of staff.

Although concerned about the enemy buildup in the north to the extent of reinforcing Khe Sanh in December with another Marine battalion, Cushman was confident that he had the situation under control. General Westmoreland, however, worried about what he perceived as a "lack of follow-up in supervision," employment of helicopters, and Marine generalship.

Vulnerable to direct attack and infiltration through the DMZ from North Vietnam to the north and from Laos to the west, I Corps, by January, resembled one large armed camp with a quarter of a million US, South Vietnamese, and allied troops deployed within its borders.

In January 1968, General Cushman received reports that the 2d NVA Division had shifted its area of operations from its base areas and was moving north towards Da Nang. In the densely populated hamlets south of the base, the men of the 1st Marine Division began to encounter stronger resistance. A Marine with a Combined Action Platoon (an experimental pacification unit that integrated a Marine squad with a South Vietnamese Popular Forces platoon) remembers how the villagers had become much more sullen, information had dried up, and almost every patrol made contact.

North of Quang Nam province in Thua Thien province, prisoner interrogations revealed the possible presence of a new North Vietnamese regiment. American commanders believed the old imperial city of Hue, the symbolic center of Vietnamese cultural and religious activity, to be a major objective of the Communist forces.

General Cushman, like General Westmoreland, looked to the north for the enemy to make his primary offensive effort. By the end of 1967, the NVA appeared to be ready to make a fresh thrust at the isolated Marine base at Khe Sanh. Although encountering little enemy opposition to his patrols in December, one Marine company commander declared that he could "smell" the enemy out there.

The NVA gave every evidence that an attack was imminent. On 2 January, a Marine listening post just outside the main perimeter of the Khe Sanh combat base reported that six men, who appeared to be dressed in Marine uniforms, were approaching the defensive wire. A Marine patrol, sent out to investigate, challenged the strangers in English and then cut down five of the six with rifle fire when one of the intruders reached for a grenade. The survivor made good his escape but documents on the five bodies revealed that all were relatively high-ranking North Vietnamese officers, including a regimental commander.

By mid-January the 304th NVA Division, an elite home guard division which had fought at Dien Bien Phu and was usually stationed near Hanoi, had

Prisoner of war —A Viet Cong ringleader and tax collector, clad in a silk shirt, pin-stripe slacks, and a brown derby is taken blindfold to a prisoner collection point for questioning. Such interrogations proved a rich source of intelligence, often revealing the movement of enemy troops.

Looking north

LOST WORLD: An aerial view of the Marine combat base at Khe Sanh. Before the siege began it was a neat piece of manmade geometry perched 1,500 feet up on a plateau in the densely forested Annamite mountain range. Three months of B-52 bombing missions quickly reduced the greenery around it to a red-brown Martian landscape.

joined the 325C Division around Khe Sanh. Two other divisions were also mentioned in US intelligence reports, the 320th NVA Division 20 miles to the northeast of Khe Sanh and the 324th Division still in Laos. The North Vietnamese had the potential to bring up about 40,000 troops supported by artillery to lay siege to the Marine base.

As part of a plan to reinforce his forces in the DMZ sector and Khe Sanh, General Cushman had implemented Operation Checkers. This moved 1st Marine Division units north from Da Nang into

Thua Thien province to relieve 3d Marine Division units posted there. On 10 January General Tompkins moved his 3d Division command post from Phu Bai near Hue to Dong Ha. Six days later, Tompkins ordered the 2d Battalion, 26th Marines to Khe Sanh.

On 20 January, an NVA lieutenant from the 325C Division defected to the Americans and reported that the enemy would attack Marine forward positions on Hill 861 and 881S after midnight and then hit the base itself. According to the defector, the overall NVA plan was to take Khe Sanh and to sweep southeast and capture Hue. A half hour after midnight, the NVA struck Hill 861. After furious fighting, the Marine positions held. At 0530 hours, the NVA followed up the ground assault with an intense bombardment of mixed caliber, including 82mm mortars, artillery rounds, and 122mm rockets. One of the rockets slammed into the Marine ammunition storage area and set off a series of secondary explosions. The Marines lost not only much of their ammunition but also most of their fuel supply.

With the action at Khe Sanh on 21 January, General Westmoreland believed that the decisive battle of the war was near. He and General Cushman agreed to reinforce the 26th Marines with yet another Marine battalion, the 1st Battalion, 9th Marines. For symbolic purposes, Westmoreland convinced the South Vietnamese command to send an ARVN airborne battalion to Khe Sanh. He also dispatched a brigade from the 1st Air Cavalry Division to reinforce the Marines in Thua Thien and Quang Tri provinces.

Although the Khe Sanh garrison consisted of more than 6,000 defenders supported by their own artillery, by the 175mm guns at Camp Carroll, and supplemented by overwhelming air superiority, General Westmoreland still had his doubts about the

OUR MAN IN WASHINGTON:
Gen. Earle G. Wheeler inspects new equipment arriving in Vietnam. As Chairman of the US Joint Chiefs of Staff from 1964-70 he was the principal military politician in Washington advancing the need for more men and supplies. Westmoreland confided in him about what he believed to be the Marines' shortcomings in standards, tactics, and command supervision.

Marine ability to hold the base. On 22 January, Westmoreland confided to Army General Earle G. Wheeler, Chairman of the US Joint Chiefs of Staff, that the Marines showed shortcomings in standards, tactics, and command supervision, which made him "feel somewhat insecure with the situation in Quang Tri Province."

Despite Westmoreland's forebodings the North Vietnamese units at Khe Sanh bided their time. For the Marines at the base, the situation at the end of January remained "enemy attack imminent." The troops filled sandbags, dug more and deeper entrenchments, and reinforced their bunkers. Their aerial resupply had already replenished their ammunition lost in the fires and explosions of 21 January. While the Marines at Khe Sanh prepared for the all-out enemy assault, the Communist forces launched their Tet offensive on 30-31 January throughout South Vietnam— everywhere but at Khe Sanh.

LONG REACH:
Artillerymen at Camp Carroll fire a 175mm gun in support of the Marines at Khe Sanh. With a range up to 20 miles, but a relative lack of accuracy compared to smaller artillery pieces, the 175mm was used most successfully for preparatory bombardments.

Warning signs

3

Preliminary attacks

THE LUNAR NEW YEAR, or Tet, was the most important of all of the Vietnamese holidays and transcended religion and class, war and peace. A time of renewal, ancestral worship, and family reunions, Tet has no counterpart in Western tradition. The celebration begins on the eve of the New Year and continues for three weeks. New Year's day and the day after were the two most significant. In 1968, the Year of the Monkey, New Year's day would be 30 January. As in previous years, most South Vietnamese believed that both sides would adhere at least to a limited extent to their self-proclaimed truces.

This Tet, however, was to be different. For months, the North Vietnamese and the Viet Cong had made preparations for their offensive in the cities. As the South Vietnamese preoccupied themselves with the forthcoming holiday, Viet Cong soldiers, disguised as civilians, slipped into the major cities. For months the Communists had smuggled weapons and ammunition into the urban areas hidden under farm produce in peasant carts or in false truck bottoms to be stored in designated "safe" storage sites until the signal was given.

Viet Cong commanders even made personal reconnaissance of projected targets in their assigned objective areas. Colonel Nam Thuyen, the commander of the 9th VC Division, pretending to be a student, visited Saigon and the bustling Tan Son Nhut Airport over the Christmas holiday. One of his regimental commanders, using the pretext of paying respects to his family dead, spent time at a family gravesite near the airport, where he carefully noted the best means of access to the base. Evoking the name of Emperor Quang Trung, who during Tet

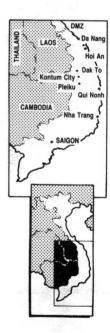

President Nguyen Van Thieu —South Vietnam's president from 1967-73. He did not believe the Communists would break the Tet truce. When they did he was away from Saigon on vacation.

1789 surprised and defeated a Chinese Army in Hanoi, the Communist leaders promised their followers victory.

Ironically, General Westmoreland kept a statuette of Quang Trung in his official residence in Saigon. Although both MACV and the South Vietnamese received numerous intelligence indicators about a forthcoming offensive, neither realized the extent or boldness of the enemy's plans. In early January, the American Embassy published the translation of a captured enemy document that directed "very strong attacks" against Saigon and other population centers. Other reports indicated attacks in the Central Highlands against Kontum City and Dak To. Aerial photography revealed that the North Vietnamese were building a road out of the A Shau valley leading towards the city of Hue. On 15 January, Westmoreland told the American Mission Council that he foresaw a 60 to 40 chance that the enemy might mount their great offensive before Tet.

On 28 January, the allies received basic confirmation of an attack on the cities. In the II Corps coastal city of Qui Nhon in Binh Dinh province, South Vietnamese security forces raided a house on a tip that local Communist cadre were meeting there. The government troops took 11 people prisoner and confiscated several tapes. Under questioning, the prisoners admitted that the Viet Cong planned to attack the city during the Tet holiday. One of the objectives would be the government radio station.

By this time, both the South Vietnamese Government and MACV had gathered additional intelligence that similar attacks were to occur in other major cities including Da Nang, Pleiku, Ban Man Thout, and Saigon. In I Corps, General Westmoreland canceled the Tet truce and the US 1st Marine Division outside of Da Nang was on full alert. Having withdrawn the bulk of his forces in III Corps from the forward border regions, the MACV commander had well over half of his forces in that Corps sector defending the immediate approaches to Saigon. Westmoreland expected the enemy to mount "a country-wide show of strength." He later admitted, however, that he believed any such "show of strength" to be limited and that the enemy would not attempt "suicidal attacks in the face of our power." Westmoreland's intelligence officer, Brigadier General Philip B. Davidson, later declared, "Even had I known exactly what was to take place, it was so preposterous that I probably would have been unable to sell it."

The South Vietnamese Government took even fewer precautions. Although supposedly canceling leaves and placing the armed forces on increased readiness, most ARVN units were at half strength during Tet. President Thieu himself had departed Saigon to spend the holidays with his wife's parents in the Mekong Delta city of My Tho.

The North Vietnamese provided other clues that this Tet season was unusual. Radio Hanoi broadcast that because of certain celestial movements of the stars and planets, the Lunar New Year would begin on 29 January rather than 30 January. Most observers later speculated that the North Vietnamese Government wanted to give their troops and people a brief respite to enjoy the Tet season.

As Tet approached, the Communists circulated among their troops an "Order of the Day" addressed to "All South Vietnam Liberation Armed Forces." The order began: "To all cadres and combatants, Move forward to achieve final victory." According to the directive, Ho Chi Minh's New Year's greeting to the Army and the population was to be considered an order to carry out the attacks. It then predicted: "This will be the greatest battle ever fought throughout the history of our country."

On 29 January, Radio Hanoi broadcast a poem that Ho Chi Minh had written for the Year of the the Monkey:

> *This Spring far outshines the previous Springs*
> *Of victories throughout the land come happy*
> *tidings.*
> *Let North and South emulate each other in*
> *fighting the US aggressors!*
> *Forward!*
> *Total Victory will be ours.*

Whether by design or by error, the Communist Military Region V began its offensive one day earlier than the rest of the country. During the first 17 hours of 30 January, Communist gunners and

Ho Chi Minh —President of North Vietnam since 1945 when he had proclaimed its independence from France, he was a charismatic father figure in the North. On the eve of Tet, Ho, then 78 and frail, addressed a rally in Hanoi exhorting his people to "even greater feats of battle." The name Ho Chi Minh was an adopted alias meaning "He Who Enlightens."

infantry initiated over 21 major incidents, including mortar and ground attacks against allied installations and several cities.

At Nha Trang, a coastal city in II Corps and the site of a Vietnamese Navy training center, a small ARVN security detachment protected the local radio station. Shortly after midnight on 30 January, one of the guards, a corporal, noticed two motorized carts pulling up to a nearby pagoda carrying several passengers, all dressed in ARVN uniforms. Something about the erstwhile soldiers looked peculiar and the guard decided to contact his headquarters. The guard radioed his superiors who told him that there should not be any other troops in the vicinity of the station. He woke up the rest of his detachment and fired a warning shot at the group at the pagoda, who returned the fire. The situation soon deteriorated into a desultory exchange of bullets between those inside and outside of the station.

A few minutes later, at about 2430 hours, six mortar shells fell near the naval training center, all missing their mark. About an hour and a half later, some 800 men of the 18B NVA Regiment launched a ground assault against the city. In a 14-hour street battle, the South Vietnamese forces with the support of American air strikes turned back the attackers

FAILED ASSAULT: Some of the Viet Cong assailants who tried to take the city of Nha Trang in the early hours of 30 January stand tagged and waiting to be interrogated. One battalion of 800 NVA troops supported the local VC. Two further battalions of reinforcements were promised but never arrived.

with heavy losses and captured several members of the local Communist infrastructure. Among the prisoners was Huynh Tung, the party political officer. Under interrogation, Tung stated that he had told his superiors that they could not capture the city with 800 men. Tung received assurances that another two battalions would reinforce the initial assault battalion. The reinforcing battalions never arrived.

At Ban Me Thuot, a city of some 65,000 people in the Central Highlands on a jungle-surrounded plateau, the Communist forces were somewhat more successful. The local populace welcomed Tet with fireworks and celebrations. At 0135 hours on the morning of the 30th, the streets were still crowded when Communist rockets and mortars fell among the revelers. Following the barrage, some 2,000 enemy troops from the 33d NVA Regiment and the

CHARGE!

A standard bearer carrying the flag of the Viet Cong (the South Vietnam People's Liberation Armed Forces) leads a VC unit in a bayonet charge during the Tet Offensive in Quang Nam province.

47

Maj. Gen. Charles P. Stone —Three weeks before Tet, troops of the 4th Infantry Division, commanded by Stone, had seized a Communist document directing an attack on Pleiku. As a result Stone stationed an additional tank company in the city.

301st VC Local Force Battalion attacked the city. Some of the Communist soldiers had mingled with the merrymakers in the streets while others came from staging positions northwest and southwest of the city. The enemy troops roamed through the streets to get at their prime military objectives, the headquarters of the 23d ARVN Division, the provincial headquarters, the treasury building, and police station. As civilians scattered before them, the Communist forces consolidated their positions in the city.

At first only the local militia reinforced by some US Special Forces fended off the first wave of assaults. By noon on the 30th, however, tanks and troops of the 8th ARVN Cavalry Squadron and the 45th ARVN Regiment mounted a counterattack against the enemy. Just southwest of the city in a small tribal Montagnard village, North Vietnamese troops rounded up and killed six American missionaries. Elsewhere in Ban Me Thuot, VC agents organized about 300 hill tribesmen to demonstrate against the government. The police, however, easily dispersed them.

At Pleiku, the mountain capital of Pleiku province and the headquarters of the II Corps command, the allies had ample forewarning of the enemy attack. On 5 January, troops of the US 4th Infantry Division under Major General Charles P. Stone had captured in the Central Highlands the Communist Liberation Army "Urgent Order Number One." This directive outlined a combined attack during Tet by the Viet Cong H-15 Battalion and the NVA 95B Regiment.

The 4th Division stationed an additional tank company in the city and General Stone shared his information with General Vinh Loc, the II Corps commander. Vinh Loc acknowledged the information and then took off in his personal aircraft to Saigon for the Tet holidays. Fortunately for the allies, the II Corps chief of staff, Colonel Le Trung Tuong, directed an increased alert on the eve of the holiday, and ordered a hesitant battalion commander, "Tet or no Tet" to place four more tanks in the city.

At 0440 hours on 30 January, a platoon of the US 173d Airborne Brigade positioned outside the city woke to the screeching sound of 122mm rockets over their heads. The American troops, who had looked forward to some rest during the supposed cease-fire, suddenly realized that the enemy gunners were only 800 meters from their positions.

In the city, confusion reigned. Communist troops from the H-15 Battalion and the 40th Sapper Battalion, dressed as ARVN soldiers, had infiltrated into the city during the night. The rocket bombardment was supposed to signal the attack, but the North Vietnamese 95B Regiment had missed the rendezvous. Waiting until almost 0930 hours before deciding to attack, the H-15th took heavy casualties trying to cross an open field. During the day, fighting occurred around the II Corps headquarters, the MACV compound in the city, a nearby US Army hospital, and the airfields. Despite the presence of both US and South Vietnamese armor units, the attack force had succeeded in penetrating the city's defenses. Only after dogged resistance, street by street and block by block, would the allies finally succeed in rooting out the remnant of the Communist attackers.

An even worse situation prevailed in the neighboring city of Kontum. At 0200 hours on the morning of the 30th after a brief mortar attack,

REST BREAK: Sky soldiers of the 173d Airborne Brigade take a break from patrolling near Pleiku. During the early hours of 30 January when the Communists launched a surprise attack on the city, a 173d platoon on rest break woke to discover the enemy only 800 meters away.

Warning signs

THE BATTLE FOR KONTUM: A scout dog and his handler from the 33d Scout Dog Platoon, 4th Infantry Division, stalk a street in Kontum to flush out enemy snipers. The city in the Central Highlands was attacked by several Communist battalions. After a week of fighting a US relief force returned Kontum to South Vietnamese control.

three to five battalions, the 304th VC Battalion, the 406th Sapper Battalion, and an undetermined number of battalions from the 406th NVA Regiment, swept into the city against limited resistance by two Montagnard scout companies and a battalion of the 42d ARVN Regiment. A composite American relief force consisting of tanks, infantrymen, and what other troops were available came to the assistance of the hard-pressed South

Vietnamese forces. The struggle for Kontum City was to witness some of the fiercest fighting of the enemy offensive.

In Qui Nhon, despite the early warnings about an attack, the South Vietnamese had not reinforced the city. About 0410 hours on the 30th, two VC battalions, one infantry and one sapper, struck and easily overwhelmed the defense forces from a Regional Forces company. The Communist troops

Warning signs

DIRECT HIT:
A petrol dump goes up in a fiery explosion during a night attack at Da Nang air base on 30 January 1968. The mortar and rocket attack was the second on the Marine airfield in 24 hours. The base had been attacked prematurely on 29 January. The attacks in the Da Nang sector provided few real gains for the Viet Cong and cost them heavy casualties.

occupied the military security building and freed the 11 cadres that had been jailed in the earlier roundup. They took prisoner the South Vietnamese Army captain who had led the successful raid. Although capturing the radio station, the Communists discovered that they had no tapes to play since they had been confiscated by the South Vietnamese. Viet Cong appeals to the population fell on deaf ears, and soon reinforcements including two South Korean infantry companies were in the city and pushing back the invaders.

Most of the attacks in Military Region V on 30 January had occurred in South Vietnam's II Corps

except for a series of assaults in I Corps near Da Nang. In an obvious premature action on 29 January, Viet Cong and North Vietnamese gunners mortared and rocketed the main air base at Da Nang and the nearby Marine helicopter airfield at Marble Mountain. During the early morning hours of 30 January, they followed this initial bombardment with another barrage of mortars and rockets on the airfields and on Marine defensive positions. In the second attack some 15 US installations came under attack, resulting in casualties and the destruction of five aircraft.

The Viet Cong followed the bombardment with

Lt. Gen. Hoang Xuan Lam —The ARVN commander in I Corps, he called for US air strikes within 200 meters of his headquarters when Viet Cong sappers came too close.

an attempt to capture the I Corps headquarters. At about 0130 hours on 30 January, a security force from the Marine 1st MP battalion intercepted a Viet Cong underwater demolitions team whose mission was to destroy the I Corps bridge across the Cau Do river. The Marines killed one enemy frogman and took the other prisoner. Shortly afterwards, elements of two Viet Cong battalions, the R-20th and the V-25th, crossed the Cau Do, but encountered stiff resistance from a Marine Combined Action Platoon and Popular Force troops in Hoa Vang district town. An enemy sapper team, however, made its way into the I Corps headquarters compound.

Colonel Nguyen Duy Hinh, the I Corps chief of staff, who lived about 500 meters from the headquarters, awoke to the exchange of automatic and small arms fire. Looking out his window, he could see the vivid colors of tracer bullets against the dark sky. He immediately telephoned Lieutenant General Hoang Xuan Lam, the I Corps commander, about the attack. In almost total disbelief, General Lam exclaimed into the telephone the Vietnamese equivalent of "baloney, baloney!" Hurriedly arriving at his headquarters carrying his everpresent black swaggerstick, General Lam called out to his US aide, Major P. S. Milantoni. He told the American officer that he wanted airstrikes and pointed with his swaggerstick at points on the map where he wanted the strikes. Somewhat taken back by the closeness of the strikes to the headquarters, Milantoni asked the I Corps commander if he was sure. Lam repeated "bomb" and use "big bombs." The American aircraft dropped bombs within 200 yards of the building causing it to shake. After the airstrikes Lam called in armed helicopters and the Viet Cong disengaged.

Some 20 miles south of Da Nang, a Communist force attacked the city of Hoi An, the provincial capital of Quang Nam province. Although taking part of the city, the VC force was unable to drive out the defenders, the ARVN 102d Engineer Battalion. Supported by American air and artillery, the engineers reinforced by the 51st ARVN Regiment forced the enemy to withdraw.

On the morning of 30 January, Lieutenant General Cushman, the commander of III MAF, airborne in his command helicopter, spotted about

200 enemy troops southeast of the air base. Cushman relayed the information to his 1st Marine Division commander, Major General Donn J. Robertson, who committed two Marine infantry battalions to the action. Poorly coordinated and poorly executed, the attacks in the Da Nang sector on 30 January resulted in heavy casualties for the Viet Cong and few gains.

Maj. Gen. Donn J. Robertson —As 1st Marine Division commander he successfully organized the defense of the air base at Da Nang.

The attacks in I and II Corps on 30 January all followed a general pattern. First incidents usually involved mortar and rocket bombardment in the early morning hours followed by a commando assault. Once inside the city, the VC shock troops married up with others who had already infiltrated into the city. Guided by local sympathizers, the attackers attempted to seize certain central facilities—a radio station, a jail, a headquarters. Once the initial force had attained a foothold, the main force troops would launch their attack. Other regular units would remain outside the cities to cut lines of communication and to exploit any opportunity. Political cadres accompanying the combat troops urged the local populace to rally to the Communist cause. Others pointed out certain "enemies of the people" to be eliminated.

Up to this point, the Viet Cong, including both guerrilla and main force units, had borne the brunt of the fighting. For the most part, the North Vietnamese regulars were held back in a reserve or exploitation role. Outside of the mortar and rocket attacks against the Da Nang air base, the thrust of the enemy attacks was directed against South Vietnamese military and administrative centers.

With the widespread violation of the Tet truce in II Corps and around Da Nang on 30 January, General Westmoreland canceled at 1100 hours the last vestiges of the cease-fire for American forces and convinced the South Vietnamese Government to do likewise. The Vietnamese canceled all leave and ordered their troops to rejoin their units. In Saigon, Westmoreland discussed the situation with his staff. His intelligence officer, General Davidson, warned the MACV commander that the spate of enemy attacks was going to spread. Westmoreland agreed, but there was little more to be done at this point. He had alerted all of his forces and all he could do was to wait for the other shoe to fall.

The battle for Saigon

4

The prime time effect

DESPITE THE ATTACKS on the 30th, Saigon celebrated the Tet holiday as if the war were on another planet. Throughout the conflict, except for isolated acts of terrorism, the South Vietnamese capital had been spared much of the bloodshed. Yet, the war was not far away. When the wind was right, residents could hear the dull boom of distant artillery. Certain hotels provided panoramic views of airstrikes on Communist strongholds in the nearby jungle. The most visible consequence of the widening war was the thousands of refugees from the countryside who had swelled the city's slum areas. Over 2 million people now crowded into Saigon, more than twice its 1963 population. Rampant inflation and a flourishing black market brought another ugly side of the war to the capital. The Tet holiday provided an excuse to forget both the bloodletting and the tawdriness of life. The night of 30 January in Saigon reverberated with the noise of firecrackers as people greeted the "Year of the Monkey."

The responsibility for the defense of Saigon had been turned over to the South Vietnamese in mid-December 1967 by the Americans as a calculated show of confidence. The ARVN had 10 battalions in and around the city supplemented by 17,000 members of the National Police. In the city, the ARVN 5th Ranger Group had the main responsibility. Two battalions of the Vietnamese General Reserve, the 1st and 8th ARVN Airborne Battalions, were slated to reinforce I Corps, but a shortage of aircraft still kept them in the Saigon region. Three Regional Force battalions rounded out the Vietnamese capital city defenses.

The American command had at its disposal a total

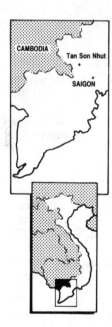

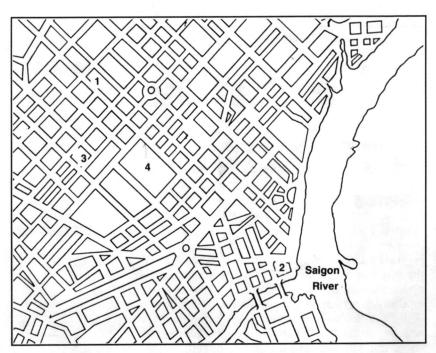

DOWNTOWN SAIGON:
The map shows
some of the
principal
buildings
involved in the
events of
January 30-31.
Key:
1. MACV HQ
2. American
Embassy
3. Chief MACV
residence
4. Presidential
Palace

of 50 maneuver battalions in III Corps, 23 in the Saigon region. In the city, the US 716th Military Police Battalion was the primary American unit. Commanded by Lieutenant Colonel Gordon D. Rowe, the MPs had responsibility for the greater Saigon area including Tan Son Nhut Airport. Dressed in starched fatigues and wearing glossy helmets emblazoned with red and white stripes and a large 716, the MPs had the mission of antiterrorist security and enforcing US military regulations. For the most part, the soldiers of the 716th spent their time escorting visiting dignitaries, writing traffic tickets, mounting guard, and assisting the Saigon Boy Scout Association. Although the 716th had an emergency plan, it was actually designed for riots and the occasional bombing. A small Marine Embassy guard provided security within the Embassy and for certain US government buildings.

General Tran Do, one of the architects of the enemy offensive, commanded the Communist forces in the Saigon region. Two Viet Cong divisions, the 5th and the 7th, were situated near the city and allied major bases at Tan Son Nhut, Long Binh, and Bien Hoa. The 7th NVA Division was to divert

American forces to the north of Saigon. Approximately 35 enemy battalions were in and around the general Saigon area.

The Viet Cong C-10 Sapper Battalion, composed of men and women from Saigon or the Saigon region, was to spearhead the Communist offensive in the city. Members of the battalion had infiltrated into the city during the past weeks. On the night of 30 January, they gathered at various predesignated rendezvous sites where the officers distributed weapons and briefed their troops on their assignments. The battalion had three main missions: to seize and hold the American Embassy, the Presidential Palace, and the radio station. Some 5,000 local force guerrillas were inside the city. Other Viet Cong units to the north, west, and south waited for the signal to reinforce the forces inside Saigon.

Just before midnight on the 30th, Viet Cong soldiers in leaf-covered conical helmets weaved through the crowded Saigon streets on their way to their objectives in the city. If any of the Tet revelers noticed them, they dismissed it as another possible coup attempt. The first mortar and rocket bursts were muffled by the noise of the fireworks. Despite all of their careful planning, however, the Communist forces launched their attacks piecemeal.

At 0130 hours on 31 January, a VC platoon from the C-10 Battalion drove up in three vehicles, including a truck loaded with explosives, to the staff entrance of the Presidential Palace on Tu Do Street. They demanded that the guards open up the gates of the Palace to the "Liberation Army" and fired B-40 antitank rockets to force their way inside. The Palace defenders, the Presidential guard reinforced by two tanks, easily repulsed the assault. At that point, 14 members of the VC platoon, 13 men and a woman, killed two US Military Policemen who happened on the scene, took the MPs' machine gun, and holed up in an unfinished high-rise building across the street from the palace. For the next two days, in front of US network TV cameras, they fought a running gun battle with ARVN soldiers, National Police, and US MPs. Only two of the original attackers survived.

In the battle for the American Embassy, the Vietnamese sappers after crashing the gate failed

Insignia of the 716th Military Police Bn —The 716th was stationed at Saigon and Tan Son Nhut throughout its service in Vietnam. During the Tet Offensive the 716th was stretched to its limit.

The battle for Saigon

REINFORCING THE GUARD: American MPs from the 716th Military Police Bn reinforce the guard at the entrance to the US Embassy compound in Saigon on 31 January 1968. Communist commandos had gained access to the Embassy compound by blasting a hole in the northeast corner of the front wall.

to enter the chancery building. The two Marines in the lobby, Sergeant Ronald W. Harper and Corporal George B. Zahuranic, had heard the rumpus outside and had quickly closed the heavy front doors of the building. The Viet Cong fired a B-40 rocket that smashed through the door and into the lobby, wounding Zahuranic and knocking Harper to the floor. On the roof, Marine Sergeant Rudy A. Soto, Jr., fired his shotgun at the VC but it jammed. Unable to raise either Harper or Zahuranic on his radio, Sergeant Soto assumed that they were dead and reported that the VC were in the building.

Captain Robert J. O'Brien, the commanding officer of the Embassy guard, roused the rest of his detachment at "Marine House," and rushed to the embassy, five blocks away.

Despite some dispute over jurisdiction, South Vietnamese police and soldiers, MPs from the 716th, and Marines quickly surrounded the Embassy compound. None knew the fate of the people inside or where the VC were except that they were inside the compound. Six Americans, including the Embassy economics officer, and two Vietnamese watchmen were in the chancery building in addition

NIGHT ATTACK:
An MP cocks an M-79 grenade launcher as military police of the 716th and the 527th MP Battalions take up their positions across the street from the Embassy as they attempt to dislodge Communist commandos who had earlier infiltrated the Embassy compound.

to the Marines. Sergeant Harper, armed with a 12-gauge shotgun, a .38 pistol, and a Beretta submachine gun, waited for the VC to burst through the door.

But the expected attack never came. Leaderless since the first exchange of fire with the MPs at the gate, the VC sappers just milled about, taking cover under huge flower pots, and returning the fire of the reaction force posted on nearby roofs and on the compound wall. After an aborted attempt, a US Army helicopter at 0800 landed troops of Company C, 502d Infantry from Bien Hoa on the chancery roof, breaking the armed stalemate at the Embassy. George Jacobson, a retired Army colonel and Embassy official, killed the last of the Viet Cong intruders in the bedroom of his villa with a pistol thrown to him through an open window.

Although the attack on the Embassy was the most dramatic and possibly the most symbolic of the Tet onslaughts in Saigon, it was basically a sideshow to other aspects of the Communist offensive. The Saigon radio station was one of the prime targets of the C-10 Battalion. The leader of the attack force, Dang Xuan Tao, had received orders in November 1967 to train a 14-man team to seize and hold the station until relieved by a VC battalion. At 0300 hours on 31 January, a jeep and two Toyotas stopped in front of the main radio studio and Tao and his commandos, dressed in police uniforms, stepped out. They shot a police guard at the door and took control of the station.

The South Vietnamese, however, had prepared a contingency plan. On a prearranged signal, the South Vietnamese transmitter station several miles away switched off power to the main studio. The VC had the main studio but could not broadcast any of their appeals. Using the transmission station the government played a strange amalgam of Viennese waltzes, the Beatles, Rolling Stones, and martial music. An ARVN airborne company finally drove the VC out from the main studio, killing most of the enemy soldiers.

At the same time a VC attack by a squad of the C-10 Battalion on the Vietnamese Navy headquarters at Bach Dang Quay proved even more of a debacle. As they approached a checkpoint, a naval guard stopped them. In the ensuing fire fight, 10 of the 12 members of the squad were killed and the other 2 captured.

In a well-coordinated attack on two Vietnamese Army encampments in the suburbs of the city, two battalions of the 101st VC Regiment successfully

ARMOR ON THE STREETS: American infantry from the 1st Bn, 18th Infantry, in an armored personnel carrier (APC) at the Vietnamese cemetery near Tan Son Nhut airport. The APC was from the 25th Infantry Division armored group that reinforced US forces at the airport from Cu Chi, the 25th's base 15 miles northwest of Saigon.

The battle for Saigon

CAPTURED: South Vietnamese troops lead away suspected Viet Cong guerrillas who participated in the aborted attack on US Bachelor Officer Quarters 3 (BOQ3) in Saigon not far from the complex housing the South Vietnamese Joint General Staff. Several American MPs who rushed to reinforce BOQ3 died in a Viet Cong ambush.

took over the Co Loa artillery base and the nearby Camp Phu Dong, the headquarters of the ARVN Armored Command. Although the enemy captured twelve 105mm howitzers at Co Loa, the ARVN gunners had removed the breech blocks from the artillery pieces, making them inoperable.

At Camp Phu Dong, the Communists again found their plans thwarted. Armor personnel from the 16th Section of COSVN accompanied the attack force, fully expecting to take over the tanks that they expected to find there. Obviously, the Communist command had been unaware that the South Vietnamese had transferred the tanks from Phu Dong nearly two months before.

In Saigon, the 716th Military Police Battalion had

its hands full. Emergency calls from Americans
scattered all through the city flooded its
switchboards. Lieutenant Colonel Rowe
implemented his "disaster plan," which largely
consisted of sending a platoon of 25 men in open
trucks to areas of trouble with only rough sketch
maps to guide them. Indiscriminate small arms and
automatic fire occurred throughout the city as
individual citizens started to defend themselves. In
one incident an aerial observer called for an artillery
mission on Viet Cong soldiers pushing mortars in
carts. Further reconnaissance revealed that the so-
called mortar men were actually early morning
golfers on the Saigon golf course.

   In a letter to his wife, Marine Brigadier General

Street fighter —An ARVN ranger fires an M-79 grenade launcher at an enemy position during the fighting in Saigon. One participant noted that explosions were accentuated by the way their sound bounced off buildings.

John R. Chaisson, who headed the MACV Combat Operations Center, provided a description of the chaos during the first few hours. Chaisson, who lived only about a half block from the Embassy, had been aroused by the first satchel charge explosion. After looking out on the confusion and firing in the street below, the Marine general took his rifle and joined the sentry at his gate. Chaisson wrote: "There is something wild about street fighting. Everything seems to be going in all directions and the big booms are accentuated by bouncing off the buildings."

At daybreak Chaisson realized that the entire city was under attack. He obtained the services of a Vietnamese Marine Sergeant to pick him up in a jeep and they made the "run" to MACV headquarters at the Tan Son Nhut air base, a distance of 3 miles. He arrived at his desk at 0730 hours that morning and immediately began to monitor the reports from all over the country coming into the Command Center. Pausing after midnight to write a letter home, he observed, "this Hq (headquarters) has been grim . . . (and) under continuous attack all day. We are all holed up here— including Westy."

Two of the most serious attacks by the Viet Cong were their efforts to overrun the large Tan Son Nhut air base, with both the MACV and Seventh Air Force headquarters located there together with the adjoining South Vietnamese Joint General Staff headquarters complex. After midnight on 31 January, three VC battalions took over the Vinatexco mill across Highway 1 from Tan Son Nhut. The enemy soldiers posted heavy machine guns in doors and windows of the factory and placed antiaircraft guns on the roof. At 0321 hours, the Viet Cong launched their three-battalion attack on the airbase. Employing B-40 rockets, mortars, and heavy automatic weapons fire, they overwhelmed the ARVN defenders of Gate 51 on the western side of the base and surged onto the airfield.

An adhoc group of defenders from the US Air Force 377th Security Police Squadron, MACV headquarters guards, and some mixed South Vietnamese units including Vice President Ky's personal guard detachment resisted the enemy advance, but eventually began to fall back. At this point, the South Vietnamese command ordered into battle the 8th ARVN Airborne Battalion, which had been waiting at Tan Son Nhut for a flight to Da Nang. The paratroopers charged over an open expanse of the airstrip, taking heavy casualties as they closed with the enemy. In fierce hand-to-hand fighting they stalled the VC advance.

In the meantime, MACV called for reinforcements for Tan Son Nhut from the US 25th Division at Cu Chi, 15 miles northwest of Saigon. A relief column of M-40 medium tanks and armored personnel carriers (APCs from Troop C, 3d Armored Squadron) sped in the early morning darkness toward the airbase. The squadron commander's personal helicopter flew overhead dropping flares to light the way. At 0600 hours, the relief force smashed into the rear of the VC at Gate 51. Despite their surprise, the Communist soldiers put up a formidable struggle. Using B-40 rockets, the VC knocked out four of the tanks and five of the APCs, nearly a third of the friendly armor. Finally about noon, the

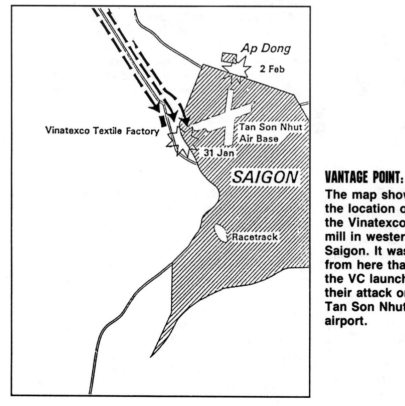

VANTAGE POINT: The map shows the location of the Vinatexco mill in western Saigon. It was from here that the VC launched their attack on Tan Son Nhut airport.

American and South Vietnamese troops in a final push drove the last VC off the airbase. The enemy retreated to the Vinatexco mill and the allied forces lay siege using both fixed-wing aircraft and helicopter gunships to support the ground troops.

Just to the east of Tan Son Nhut, VC units had also penetrated the South Vietnamese Joint General Staff (JGS) complex. On the night of 30-31 January, a Viet Cong commando team occupied the Long Hoa pagoda, across the street from Gate 5 on the southern side of the compound. At 0200 hours, a bus with the rest of the team stopped outside the gate which had just been opened to allow a South Vietnamese general to enter. The sapper team immediately rushed the gate, hoping to get inside before the ARVN guard could close it. An American MP jeep patrol suddenly came upon the scene. Distracted, the VC turned their guns on the Americans. The South Vietnamese guard at the entrance successfully closed the heavy steel gate doors and opened fire on the VC.

Although botched by the VC, the attack on Gate 5 indirectly was to result in some of the heaviest casualties for the 716th MP Battalion. The VC retreated to the Long Hoa Pagoda and exchanged fire with the ARVN guards and US MPs guarding the nearby BOQ 3 (bachelor officer quarters). The MPs requested reinforcements and the 716th dispatched a platoon to assist in the fighting. As the troop-laden truck and its two escort jeeps passed through a narrow alley at about 0400 hours near BOQ 3, the VC sprang a carefully laid ambush. A B-40 rocket took out the truck while enemy machine guns and small arms raked the jeeps with a deadly cross fire. A few survivors made their way out and called for further assistance. A claymore mine explosion prevented a rescue ambulance from getting into the alley. Sixteen MPs from the 716th died in the alley and 21 were wounded. Some of the casualties were from two relief groups that fought their way into the alley to bring out the dead and wounded.

At 0700 hours the VC attempted another assault on the Joint General Staff compound. Supposed to coordinate its attack to occur simultaneously with that of the C-10 on Gate 5, the 2d Independent Battalion arrived five hours late at its objective,

No hiding place —A soldier from the 1st Bn, 18th Infantry, 1st Infantry Division, searches a Saigon cemetery for Viet Cong snipers during the Tet Offensive.

Gate 4, in the northeastern sector of the complex. Despite its delay and the warning the earlier attack had given the South Vietnamese, the enemy were still able to quickly blast through the gate and overwhelm the relatively weak defending forces, which fell back into the compound. With victory in its grasp, the VC battalion occupied two buildings, the Vietnamese Armed Forces Language School and the headquarters of the Headquarters Company and set up defensive positions rather than extending its control. Apparently confused by the elaborate sign markings reading "General Headquarters Company," the Viet Cong mistakenly thought they had captured the main building housing the headquarters of the Vietnamese Joint General Staff. Given this reprieve, the South Vietnamese brought up two Airborne battalions, reinforced later by a Vietnamese Marine battalion, and more tanks. After dogged combat, the South Vietnamese forces finally cleared the VC out of the JGS compound.

With the fighting still continuing, a US helicopter landed in the JGS complex about noon, bringing President Thieu back from My Tho. In his absence, Vice President Ky had about three hours earlier broadcast an appeal for the people in the city to

AFTERMATH: American Ambassador to the Republic of Vietnam, Ellsworth Bunker, (partially obscured by the MP in the foreground) inspects the damage to the Embassy with several of his senior aides. During the attack the ambassador had been taken to a prearranged hiding place for his safety.

remain calm. Now Thieu called a meeting of his cabinet in the JGS headquarters to assess the situation while gunfire could still be heard less than a kilometer away.

The US military and civilian leadership in Saigon also had begun its evaluation of the situation. General Westmoreland, who had been awoken when the first reports of the enemy assaults arrived in the early morning hours of 31 January, listened in astonishment at his residence on Tran Quy Cap Street to telephone briefings about the scope of the enemy offensive. Nearly every city in South Vietnam appeared to be under attack. The Viet Cong had thrown three battalions at Tan Son Nhut Airport, the site of his own MACV headquarters. Even more unbelievable, the American Embassy was under attack. An Embassy security force

The battle for Saigon

ARVN ELITE:
Members of Co A, 30th Ranger Bn, maintain radio contact as they move in against Viet Cong guerrillas. The ARVN Rangers were considered an elite unit and successive South Vietnamese leaders, who wanted their best troops nearby to guarantee their own security, always kept a company stationed in Saigon.

already had spirited Ambassador Bunker from his residence to a prearranged hiding place for his safekeeping. After the action at the Embassy was over, General Westmoreland and his aide drove there to praise the efforts of the Marines and the MPs.

In Saigon, by afternoon, the situation had begun to clarify. Although fires were burning, bombs were dropping, and the sharp staccato sound of machine guns could be heard throughout much of the city, the enemy offensive appeared to be stalled. At both Tan Son Nhut and the Joint General Staff compound, the VC attacking forces were fighting rearguard actions. The enemy, however, had succeeded in establishing a foothold in the northern suburbs and much of the southern and western precincts of the city, including Cholon. He had seized

the Phu Tho race track, which he made into his Saigon command post. Although General Westmoreland later dismissed the race track as militarily insignificant, it was situated near an important road junction leading into Cholon, it was easily identifiable for troops unfamiliar with the city, and its occupation prevented its use as a helicopter landing zone by the allied forces.

General Westmoreland had hoped that the South Vietnamese could defend the capital without the assistance of major American reinforcements. The South Vietnamese soldiers, Marines, and National Police with the support of American fixed-wing aircraft and helicopter gunship support had succeeded in stabilizing the situation. Yet, the ARVN had exhausted their reserve and were spread too thin to take the offensive. Westmoreland agreed reluctantly to bring American infantry into the Saigon fighting. On 31 January, he committed five US battalions in and around Saigon, with some of the heaviest action for the Americans near the Phu Tho race track.

After futile attempts by South Vietnamese units to retake the track from the 6th VC Local Battalion, the American command ordered Brigadier General Robert C. Forbes, the commander of the 199th Light Infantry Brigade, to send US reinforcements into the fight. A task force, built around Company A, 3d Battalion, 7th Infantry, moved into the city in eight APCs from the Brigade Reconnaissance Squadron and several trucks. Six blocks from the track the VC opened up on the convoy with small arms and automatic weapons fired from the roof tops and windows of surrounding buildings. The column pushed ahead for two more blocks against increasing enemy resistance. At this point, a VC gunner stopped the column with a B-40 rocket that smashed into the lead APC, setting it on fire.

The American infantrymen dismounted from their vehicles and began to clear out the buildings on either side. Using Recoilless Rifles, M-79 grenade launchers, and single-shot LAWs (light antitank weapons) to clear the way, the US troops fought their way house-by-house toward their objective. Huey helicopter gunships supported the ground troops with repeated salvos of their miniguns and rockets upon the enemy. After heavy and bloody street fighting, the Viet Cong finally fell back to defensive positions in the park surrounding the track.

The American company attempted a frontal assault against the Communist position, but fell back in the face of automatic weapons and rifle fire. The US commander decided upon another course of action. Under cover of the Huey gunships and fusillades of recoilless rifle rounds, the American company circled the VC and came upon them from the rear. Taken by surprise and unable to withstand the overwhelming American fire superiority, the Viet Cong battalion broke and ran, leaving the race track for the time being to the Americans. After dark, US helicopters airlifted two more companies of the battalion into the race track area. Heavy fighting still faced the 3d Battalion as it attempted to expand its perimeter out from the race track. The following day, General Westmoreland would bring two more US battalions into the battle for Saigon.

After the first day's fighting in Saigon, the Viet Cong were on the defensive. They had failed to obtain their main objectives and the people had not rallied to their cause. Indeed, as the American and South Vietnamese troops advanced into the Viet Cong held areas, thousands of refugees streamed past looking for sanctuary in the government-held districts. Although still facing a bloody struggle in Saigon, Westmoreland turned his attention to the situation outside the city as he and his staff tried "to stay on top of literally hundreds of actions" that had erupted throughout the country.

Behind the barricades —An ARVN Ranger uses a street vendor's stall as temporary cover during the fighting in Cholon, the Chinese quarter of Saigon, where the VC had gained a foothold.

All-out assault

The Tet Offensive nationwide

IN THEIR TET OFFENSIVE launched on 30-31 January, the Communists sent an estimated 64,000 to 84,000 troops into action the length and breadth of South Vietnam. They hit 36 of the provincial capitals, 5 of the 6 autonomous cities, 64 of the 242 district capitals, and over 50 hamlets. For the most part, like the attacks on 30 January in Military Region V, the Communist forces avoided the American forces and directed the full thrust of their offensive against the South Vietnamese.

The Saigon region was the exception to the general pattern. The Communists attacked the American Embassy in the city and the large Tan Son Nhut complex. Fifteen miles to the north, the enemy also struck the Long Binh base, the headquarters of General Weyand, the II Field Force commander. At 0300 hours on 31 January a large explosion rocked the entire base as the 5th VC Division launched its offensive with a 122mm rocket attack against Long Binh and the nearby Bien Hoa airfield, the headquarters of South Vietnam's ARVN III Corps.

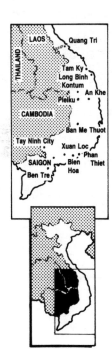

At Long Binh, the VC followed the rocket attack with a ground assault. The 275th VC Regiment supported by a local force battalion attacked the main base. Another local force battalion hit the eastern perimeter, diverting attention from enemy sappers who had infiltrated the ammunition supply dump. Troops from the US 199th Light Infantry Brigade and from a mechanized battalion of the US 9th Infantry Division supported by helicopter gunships repulsed the initial thrust, inflicting heavy losses upon the enemy. Despite attempts by US Army demolitions experts to remove all of the charges, four pallets of ammunition exploded, shaking the buildings on the base.

Coordinated attacks —This official map, published by the US Military Assistance Command, Vietnam, (MACV), shows the pattern of the Tet attacks on 30-31 January 1968.

In the II Field Force Tactical Center Lieutenant General Weyand calmly studied his situation map and ordered the movement of US forces to meet the enemy onslaught. Army helicopters brought Company B, 4th Battalion, 39th Infantry, into a "hot" landing zone right across from the American headquarters building. With both air and artillery support, the US infantry troops cleared the immediate area and pushed the Viet Cong back into an adjacent village. By nightfall, the Americans had thrown the Viet Cong out of the neighboring hamlets and the fight for Long Binh was largely over. The US 11th Armored Cavalry had arrived after a 12-hour road march to provide additional security.

At Binh Hoa, the Viet Cong followed the same tactics as they did at Long Binh. After a 24-rocket barrage, the 274th VC Regiment launched a ground assault. A mixed group of US MPs and South Vietnamese troops prevented the VC from reaching the airfield. At dawn, Army helicopters brought in the 2d Battalion, 506th Infantry (2/506) to reinforce the hard-pressed defenders. With the III Corps Headquarters under attack by another VC local force battalion, General Weyand sent a mechanized column from Long Binh down Route 1. The APCs after heavy fighting managed to join 2/506 at Bien Hoa. By 1 February, units from the 11th Armored Cavalry had reinforced 2/506 and cleaned out the last enemy pocket of resistance in the Bien Hoa-Long Binh sector.

Elsewhere in III Corps the enemy hit Ben Cat and Duc Hoa on 31 January, and, the next day, struck at the ARVN engineering school at Phu Cuong and the cites of Cu Chi and Ba Ria. The 3d Battalion of the Royal Australian Regiment led an ARVN relief force to retake the latter city. At Xuan Loc, the headquarters of the 18th ARVN Division, the South Vietnamese supported by artillery and heavy American air strikes beat back the attackers. On the night of 3 February, the Viet Cong struck again in the Bien Hoa area, this time at the Newport Bridge between Bien Hoa and Saigon. Although the 273d VC Regiment succeeded in capturing the eastern edge of the bridge, US MPs and a unit of the 5th ARVN Cavalry Squadron retook the span in heavy fighting. Three days later another Viet Cong force attacked Tay Ninh City. This time the South Vietnamese were ready: they ambushed the lead VC column and US helicopter gunships finished the job, routing the VC, who left behind banners they planned to carry in the victory parade.

In I Corps on 31 January, the offensive had spread to the cities in the northern two provinces of Quang Tri and Thua Thien. Unlike the fighting in the other Corps areas, North Vietnamese regulars played a large role. Two NVA regiments captured most of Hue City in probably the enemy master stroke of the entire offensive. Further north, in Quang Tri City, the enemy assault fell short of the hoped-for success. In the early morning hours of 31 January, the 812th NVA Regiment and the 10th VC Sapper Battalion attacked the city, but the 1st ARVN Regiment supported by the 9th ARVN Airborne Battalion made a valiant defense.

At nearby Camp Evans, Colonel Donald V. Rattan, commander of the 1st Brigade of the 1st Cavalry Division, which had been sent north for the possible relief of Khe Sanh, agreed to assist the South Vietnamese troops in Quang Tri. In a two-battalion helicopter assault out of a dense fog, the 1st Brigade struck at the rear of the North Vietnamese force. By the afternoon of 1 February, the fighting was over and the North Vietnamese had lost more than 400 men.

On 31 January, in the southern provinces of I Corps and in II Corps, the Communists continued the series of attacks that they had prematurely launched the day before. South of Da Nang, Marines, ARVN troops, and Korean Marines fought off the attacks by the VC R20 and V-25 Local Force Battalions and several local force companies. The 7th Marines fended off an assault by the 31st VC Regiment in the western An Hoa region and Marine reconnaissance "Stingray" teams called in artillery and air strikes on units of the 2d NVA Division advancing into the Da Nang area. On 31 January, NVA gunners mortared the Marble Mountain helicopter air facility once more. During the next few days, the Communists limited themselves to mortar and rocket attacks, but American and South Vietnamese intelligence received reliable reports that the 2d NVA Division was preparing for another ground assault.

Gen. Tran Van Tra —The deputy chief of staff of the Viet Cong, he is thought to have slipped in to VC headquarters near Saigon a month before Tet to inspire his forces.

All-out assault

THE BATTLE OF THU DUC: A machine gunner with the the 28th Infantry fires a burst from his M-60 at VC main force troops in the hamlet of Thu Duc, not far from the Newport Bridge, the scene of exceptionally heavy fighting during Tet.

Further south, on the 31st, two VC battalions struck at the city of Tam Ky, the capital of Quang Tin province, mortared Chu Lai, the headquarters of the Americal Division, and then six battalions launched an attack on Quang Ngai City, the headquarters of the 2d ARVN Division. In all three cases, allied air and ground units easily overcame the VC forces. In a throwback to more primitive warfare, a 700-man VC guerrilla force armed with spears and knives as well as rifles overran the Ba To District Headquarters in Quang Ngai province. The VC burned the district chief's house, and then disappeared, leaving behind several of their spears and one carbine.

In II Corps, like I Corps, on 31 January, the Viet Cong extended their campaign to new sectors that

had not come under attack the day before. On the 31st, the Viet Cong hit Bong Son, a coastal city in northern II Corps, An Khe in the Central Highlands, and the city of Phan Thiet on the coast in southern II Corps. Only in Phan Thiet, of the three, did it take the allies more than a day to repel the assault.

At 0300 hours on the 31st, the 840th Main Force VC Battalion and the 402d Local Force VC Battalion struck the MACV compound in Phan Thiet, the water point, and the local sector headquarters. The US 3d Battalion, 506th Infantry, came to the assistance of the ARVN 44th Regiment in countering the enemy attacks. By 4 February, the allied units had cleared most of the city, but skirmishing continued for six more days.

Hard-fought battles in the cities of Pleiku, Ban

THE COMBAT ZONE:
A US armored personnel carrier from Long Binh passes through Bien Hoa. The open shells and remnants of buildings provide gruesome monuments to the fierce fighting. US forces destroyed buildings to deny the Viet Cong hiding places.

Me Thuot, and Kontum, all attacked on the 30th, lasted for several days. On 1 February, shortly after midnight, the Viet Cong 145th and 186th Battalions attacked the mountain resort town of Da Lat in the highlands and the site of the Vietnamese military academy. The assistant province chief rallied two undermanned Regional Force companies and a company of freshman cadets in a spirited defense. On 5 February, US Special Forces units and the 11th ARVN Ranger Battalion reinforced the defenders and six days later finally secured the city.

Throughout II Corps, the Communists in their Tet offensive launched attacks against 7 of the 12 provincial capitals, and over 10 ground assaults. Although the subordinate ARVN units fought reasonably well, the South Vietnamese II Corps generalship left much to be desired. General Vinh Loc, the II Corps commander, came back from Saigon to Pleiku on the afternoon of 31 January. He immediately led an ARVN platoon against a small

VC force that occupied his house. While Loc concerned himself with the protection of his personal property, US Army Colonel J. W. Barnes, the chief American liaison officer, asked the general to take charge of his headquarters and focus his attention on the overall Corps situation. Shouting that he was not an "American corporal," but the "II Corps general in command," Loc returned to his headquarters, but refused to have any dealings with Barnes. The South Vietnamese Joint General Staff later removed Loc from his command and made him Commandant of the South Vietnamese National Defense College.

In IV Corps, which contained the populous Mekong Delta, the South Vietnamese suffered from the same lack of leadership. Striking in 13 of the 16 provinces in the Delta during the first 48 hours of Tet, the Communists achieved almost complete surprise despite the earlier warnings. Major General Nguyen Van Manh, the IV Corps Commander, barricaded himself in his mansion, while for all practical purposes, his American advisors ran the war. Viet Cong units captured most of Ben Tre, the capital of Kien Hoa peninsula and part of Chau Doc, the capital of Chau Doc province. They had also launched heavy attacks against the Delta cities of Cai Be, Cai Lay, Can Tho, My Tho, Soc Trang, Truc Giang, and Vinh Long. The VC had cut Route 4, the major road in the Delta, in 62 places and blew up six bridges.

Although the South Vietnamese largely were responsible for the Delta, the US 9th Infantry Division provided one brigade that operated together with the ships of US Navy Task Force 117 as the US riverine force in the upper Delta region. During the Tet offensive, the riverine force came to the relief of the ARVN 7th Division in My Tho and the 9th ARVN Division in Vinh Long. In My Tho, three VC battalions came within 700 yards of the 7th Division command post, before being turned back in stubborn house-to-house combat. It took four days, from 4 to 8 February, for the riverine troops and the South Vietnamese to clear Vinh Long.

In the Delta, like the rest of Vietnam, American firepower and airpower eventually routed the Viet Cong—but at a cost. In one of the memorable quotes of the war, an American major told one news

Bridge guard —A South Vietnamese Ranger from the 30th Ranger Bn on 31 January 1968 guarding the Newport Bridge on Route 1 between Bien Hoa and Saigon. A few days later a VC regiment succeeded in capturing part of the span before being repulsed by South Vietnamese and US troops.

All-out assault

MOPPING UP:
After the Viet Cong attack on the II Field Force headquarters at Long Binh, armored personnel carriers from the US 9th Infantry Division roll over the debris of destroyed homes as they advance toward a pocket of enemy resistance just 250 meters from the large Long Binh facility.

correspondent, "It became necessary to destroy the town (Ben Tre) in order to save it." Civilian casualties were heavy in the Delta region: 2,400 killed, 5,000 wounded, and more than 211,000 people were left homeless. The South Vietnamese claimed they had killed 5,200 of the guerrillas and took 560 prisoners.

By 6 February, South Vietnam had weathered the first wave of the Communist offensive. Its army had not deserted in the face of the enemy, but, for the most part, stood its ground and fought back. Even the despised local militias, the Regional and Popular Forces, gave a good account of themselves.

Yet, the Vietnamese had shown several weaknesses. Despite ample warning of a possible offensive during Tet, including the attacks in I and II Corps on 30 January, the South Vietnamese were caught by surprise. In fact one former ARVN officer later wrote, "the surprise was total." More importantly, however, ARVN officers had shown little initiative. While ARVN soldiers fought well in defensive positions, they were slow to counterattack and to take the offensive. Very often they waited for American airpower, infantry combat forces, and overwhelming supporting fires before clearing areas occupied by fairly small Viet Cong

groups. Nevertheless, the Communists were now on the defensive and the supposed uprising of the people never occurred.

In the II, III, and IV Corps areas, the allies had entered the mopping up stage in most of the urban areas. Only in Saigon did the Viet Cong forces still hold onto significant parts of the city, including the Cholon area. The VC would strike mostly at night, and very often during the day mix with the rest of the citizenry. Several Communist "hit squads" went through the neighborhoods they controlled and eliminated so-called "enemies of the people." Like most wars, both sides had committed cruelties against one another. In one of the most remarkable images of the war, Associated Press photographer Eddie Adams and an NBC television crew caught

with their cameras the South Vietnamese police chief, Brigadier General Nguyen Ngog Loan, executing in cold blood with one pistol shot an unarmed and bound VC prisoner. The prisoner, a Viet Cong officer, before being captured, had ordered the death of one of Loan's most trusted subordinates and his entire family including the children.

With five Airborne battalions, five Marine Battalions, and five Ranger Battalions in the city, supported by artillery, the South Vietnamese Joint General Staff developed its plans to eradicate the VC from Saigon. While the operation was supposed to be largely a South Vietnamese show, the Joint General Staff asked for American reinforcements. In renewed heavy fighting around the Phu Tho race track, the 3d Battalion, 7th Infantry on 11 February

ASSORTED SPOILS: US troops sort through enemy gear left behind after the failed attack on Long Binh. This odd assortment of web equipment, medicines, ammunition, documents, and food revealed little uniformity in the enemy's means of supply.

All-out assault

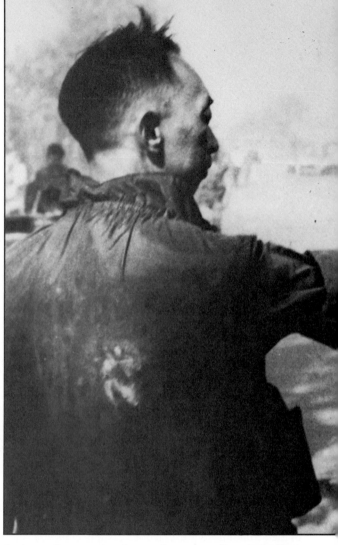

IN COLD BLOOD:
This remarkable execution scene showing South Vietnamese police chief Brig. Gen. Nguyen Ngog Loan executing with one shot an unarmed and bound VC prisoner has become one of the most enduring images of the Vietnam War. Taken during Tet, the photograph ricocheted round the world and reinforced the growing antiwar belief that the US was propping up a corrupt and ruthless regime. The furor obscured the fact that the prisoner, a Viet Cong officer, had once ordered the death of one of Loan's most trusted men and his entire family, including the children.

destroyed an enemy forward command post. At first the allies believed they might have killed General Tran Do, who commanded the Viet Cong forces in Saigon. This later proved to be untrue, but the US and Vietnamese forces continued their advance against pockets of Viet Cong in the Cholon sector. General Westmoreland, by this time, believed that the situation in Saigon and the lower three Corps areas was relatively under control.

He was less sanguine about the situation in I Corps. The battle still raged for Hue City and the Marines in the eastern DMZ continued to meet

Eddie Adams (AP)

strong resistance in their efforts to keep the Cua Viet logistic lifeline open. Westmoreland also remained worried about the Marines at Khe Sanh. On 5 February a Marine company repulsed a strong enemy effort to take Hill 861A, one of the Marine outposts protecting the main base. In the early morning hours of 7 February, a North Vietnamese regiment, supported by nine PT-76 Soviet-built amphibious tanks in the first Communist use of armor in the south, overran the US Special Forces Camp at Lang Vei, 5 miles west of Khe Sanh. Because of the rugged terrain and fearing an

COUNTERATTACK:
Troops and armored personnel carriers from the US 9th Infantry Division advance upon the enemy just outside of Long Binh, the headquarters of the US II Field Force, 15 miles north of Saigon. The VC 275th Regiment had launched its attack against this major American facility in the early hours of 31 January 1968.

ambush, the Marine command decided against sending a relief force to Lang Vei.

Further south, the 2d NVA Division launched a series of attacks south of Da Nang, primarily aimed at the ARVN 51st Regiment and Marine Combined Action Platoons with the Popular Forces. Two Marine battalions, the 2d Battalion, 3d Marines, and the 3d Battalion, 5th Marines, protecting the approaches to Da Nang, provided reaction forces that together with air and artillery support beat back the enemy assaults. The two battalions accounted for over 350 NVA casualties. Despite their success, the Marine forces at Da Nang were spread thin.

Concerned that the enemy was possibly about to make an all-out effort in I Corps and angry that the Marines had made no effort to relieve Lang Vei, General Westmoreland, on 7 February, visited General Cushman in the III MAF Headquarters at Da Nang. At the commander's conference, Major General Donn J. Robertson, the commander of the 1st Marine Division, briefed Westmoreland on the situation at Da Nang and stated that he needed more troops. The MACV commander then turned to Major General Samuel Koster, the commander of the Americal Division, and told him to reinforce the 1st Division with two to four battalions from the

Americal. Koster and Robinson then left the meeting to work out the details. Westmoreland later complained that Cushman and his staff "appeared complacent, seemingly reluctant to use the Army forces I had put at their disposal." Cushman, on the other hand, claimed that although the Americal Division was under his nominal operational control, he dared not move any battalion unless he first had the concurrence of MACV.

In any event, General Westmoreland continued to have reservations about the ability of the Marine command to handle the situation in I Corps. As one member of the MACV staff wrote, "Cushman has been pedestrian—not bad, just pedestrian." The MACV commander decided at this point to establish a temporary MACV (Forward) headquarters under his deputy, the blunt-speaking former tank commander, General Creighton W. Abrams, at Phu Bai to coordinate the war in the northern two provinces of Quang Tri and Thua Thien. Although an uncomfortable command relationship, it did not result in the total shake-up of the northern command that many Marines feared.

As both MACV and III MAF looked north, the major battle of the Tet offensive began to take shape—not at Khe Sanh or the DMZ front—but in the heretofore peaceful city of Hue.

THE ATTACK CONTINUES: Enemy mortars and rockets destroyed this C-47 transport aircraft at Tan Son Nhut air base. It was one of a series of attacks that the Communists mounted against Saigon and the vicinity in mid-February. Despite the damage shown here, these later attacks lacked the coordination and intensity of the earlier action.

The struggle for Hue

HUE WAS THE MOST Vietnamese of all of the large cities. For years it had been the intellectual and cultural center of Vietnam. Many of the top leaders on both sides of the war were graduates of the city's famed Quoc Hoc High School. These included Ngo Dinh Diem, the former President of the Republic of Vietnam, and Ho Chi Minh, the President, Vo Nguyen Giap, the Defense Minister, and his politburo colleague Pham Van Dong, the premier of the Democratic Republic of Vietnam. It was from Hue that Thich Tri Quang began the Buddhist agitation that eventually resulted in the overthrow of Diem. Hue was again the center of antigovernment protests in the spring of 1966 against the military regime of Thieu and Ky. The aborted 1966 "Struggle Movement" led to constitutional and electoral reforms, but the Thieu government viewed Hue and its university as a bastion of dissent.

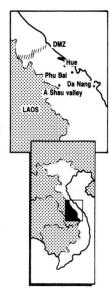

Despite its former eminence in Vietnamese politics and life, Hue could be called the city the war forgot. It brought to mind both the past glories of the Nguyen dynasty and the more recent French colonial era. Divided by the Huong or "River of Perfumes," Hue was literally two cities.

North of the river was the Citadel, the fortified city built by the emperor Gia Long in the early nineteenth century. Giving the appearance of a medieval walled city with its water-filled moats, the Citadel covered a three-square-mile area. High ramparts and towers defied any would-be conqueror.

Inside the walls lay oriental gardens, temples, pagodas, and the Imperial Palace with its large gilt and dragon-decorated throne room of the Vietnamese Emperors. The sounds of gongs and Buddhist bonzes and nuns chanting their prayers often reverberated through the streets of the old city.

The more modern city lay south of the river. About half the size of the Citadel, it formed a rough triangle outlined by the Perfume River and the Phu Cam Canal. Southern Hue contained the University, the stadium, the hospital, the prison, and the

government buildings. The Cercle-Sportif with its veranda overlooking the river brought back memories of the French colonial administration. Vietnamese girls garbed in their traditional *Ao Dai* evoked the exotic as they walked or bicycled along stately Le Loi Boulevard, which paralleled the riverfront.

According to Vietnamese legend, the Lotus flower rising out of the mud of the river symbolized Hue. Like the lotus, Hue represented serenity and peace amidst chaos. The realities of the Vietnam War

THE BATTLEGROUND: An aerial view of the Perfume River at Hue, looking west. The walled Citadel with its 3-square-mile interior containing the Imperial Place is on the right.

A PLACE IN HISTORY: The fortified walls of the Citadel contained oriental gardens, temples, pagodas and tombs like these that were the last resting places of the Nguyen monarchs who ruled Vietnam intermittently for nearly two centuries. Once the capital city, Hue embodied Vietnam's historic past.

seldom disturbed the residents of this city of 140,000. This Tet, however, was to be different. Two North Vietnamese regiments stood ready to strike at the former imperial capital.

On 30 January 1968, the 4th and 6th North Vietnamese Army Regiments, having come out of their mountain bastions, waited on the approaches to the city for the signal to attack. The 6th NVA, with its three battalions and the attached 12th VC Sapper Battalion, had as its main objectives the 1st ARVN Division Headquarters, the Tay Loc airfield, and Imperial Palace, all in the old city. To the south, the 4th NVA Regiment was to attack the MACV compound, and capture the prison and the Thua Thien provincial headquarters in the modern quarter.

By 30 January, members of the sapper battalion together with VC local forces had infiltrated inside the city, mingling with the crowds of Vietnamese that came to Hue for the Tet holiday. Outside of the city, at 1700 hours, the lead unit of the 6th NVA had left the jungle and reached Hill 138. According to a North Vietnamese report, the troops ate a meal of dumplings, tet cakes, dried meat, and glutenous rice mixed with sugar. Many of the soldiers changed into new uniforms and poured tea into their canteens. At 2000 hours, the regiment divided into three separate assault groups and began its advance upon the city.

At 0230 hours on 31 January, the North Vietnamese commander waited in his improvised command post waiting for word that the attack had begun. He had directed that the first rockets hit the city at 0230 hours. A forward observation post reported: "I am awake, I am looking down at Hue ... the lights of the city are still on, the sky is quiet, and nothing is happening."

Inside the Citadel, four Viet Cong soldiers, dressed in South Vietnamese Army uniforms, moved to take over a guard post protecting one of the gates leading into the inner city. At 0233 hours as the signal flare lit up the sky, the VC killed the ARVN troops at the gate and signaled with their flashlights for the NVA to come in. Under cover of rockets and mortars, similar scenes were repeated throughout the city.

Although allied intelligence showed signs of an enemy buildup of strength and increased activity in the A Shau valley, only 40 miles southwest of the city, neither the Vietnamese nor American commands expected a major thrust at Hue City itself. Brigadier General Ngo Quang Truong, the commanding officer of the 1st ARVN Division, aware of the enemy attacks on Da Nang the previous day, canceled all leave and kept his full complement at the headquarters compound and positioned his all-volunteer "Black Panther" Company at the Tay Loc airfield. None of his other units were in the city.

The US Marine command was even in more disarray in the Hue sector. Responding to the perceived threat to Khe Sanh and the DMZ, the Marines inaugurated Operation Checkers, moving all of the 3d Marine Division to Quang Tri province. The 1st Marine Division was to take over the 3d Marine Division command post at Phu Bai, about 7-8 miles southeast of Hue.

At the end of January, Operation Checkers was in full swing. The 1st Marine Division Task Force X-Ray, under Brigadier General Foster C. LaHue, assumed control of the Phu Bai sector. LaHue had under him two infantry regimental headquarters, the 1st and 5th Marines, but only three battalions. Although located near Hue, the responsibility of the defense of the city lay entirely with the South Vietnamese. The Marine command at Phu Bai had

Brig. Gen. Ngo Quang Truong —As commanding officer of the 1st ARVN Division he attended the flag-raising ceremony at the Citadel on 30 January to mark the Year of the Monkey. Shortly after he received reports of the enemy attacks on Da Nang and placed his forces on alert.

almost no intelligence at all on the situation in Hue.

In Hue, the South Vietnamese during the early hours of 31 January put up a valiant defense with the limited resources they had on hand. The 802d and the 800th Battalions of the 6th NVA Regiment entered the western gate and pushed north towards the 1st ARVN Division headquarters compound. At the Tay Loc airfield, the Black Panther Company met the the 800th with a volley of LAW rockets and stopped the enemy. Captain Tran Ngoc Hue, the Black Panther commander, received orders, however, to withdraw to the headquarters and help with the defense of that compound.

In the initial surprise, the 802d NVA Battalion penetrated the division compound, but an ad hoc group of clerks led by staff officers forced the attackers back. With the arrival of the Black Panthers the division compound successfully repulsed the continuing assaults by the enemy battalion.

Outside of the 1st Division headquarters compound, however, the North Vietnamese successfully controlled almost all of the Citadel. At 0800 hours, NVA soldiers raised the yellow-starred flag of the National Liberation Front above the fortress gate of the old city.

The insignia of the all-volunteer "Black Panther" Company that Truong deployed at Tay Loc airfield.

Much the same situation existed in the modern city. At the MACV compound, US advisors woke up to the sound of enemy 122mm rockets and 82mm mortars landing inside. Units of the 4th NVA Regiment supported by local forces and sappers followed with a ground assault. Although surprised, like the 1st Division staff across the river, the Americans grabbed whatever weapons they could find and took up defensive positions. The advisors threw back the initial enemy onslaught with heavy losses. While not making further ground assaults, the North Vietnamese maintained a virtual siege of the American compound with mortars, rockets, and automatic weapons fire, Outside of the MACV compound and the Navy LCU (Landing Craft, Utility) ramp to the northwest of the compound, the southern portion of the city, like the Citadel, was largely under Communist control.

Answering an appeal for assistance and knowing nothing of the situation in Hue on 31 January, Brigadier General LaHue at 0830 hours sent his

only reserve, Company A, 1st Battalion, 1st Marines, to the city to relieve the MACV compound. Marine Captain Gordon D. Batcheller ordered his understrength company into trucks and started for Hue on Route 1. Two Army dusters, trucks with four mounted .50 caliber machine guns, headed and brought up the rear of the convoy. Enroute, the company came upon four Marine M-48 tanks from the 3d Tank Battalion on their way to the Hue ramp for further transhipment north. Accompanying the tanks was Lieutenant Colonel Edward J. LaMontagne, the embarkation officer of the 3d Marine Division. LaMontagne decided to join forces with the Marine company.

Just outside of Hue, the Marines met their first resistance. As the convoy passed through a village on the outskirts of the city, enemy snipers opened fire. Batcheller's troops returned the fire as the trucks and tanks rolled through the town. The reinforced company then crossed the An Cuu bridge across the Phu Cam canal.

Once on the other side, Batcheller ordered his troops to dismount from the trucks and to use the tanks for cover. Both sides of the street were lined with clusters of closely-grouped buildings. The street was absolutely quiet. Riding on the lead tank, Batcheller led the Marines through a gauntlet of fire

THE OPPOSITION:
Viet Cong forces in action at Hue during the Tet Offensive. The VC in the center is firing a Soviet-design RPD light machine gun. His companions are firing AK-47s.

Hanging in —A Marine takes cover behind a garden wall during the battle of Hue. The enemy's determination to hang on to Hue made it one of the bitterest battles of the war.

from small arms and automatic weapons as well as B-40 antitank rockets. Forced to a halt by the heavy enemy fire, the Marines fought back as well as they could. Batcheller lay wounded, bleeding profusely from several wounds after failing to rescue a wounded Navy corpsman. Gunnery Sergeant J. L. Canley, a Black Marine and a giant of a man, over 6 feet 4 inches tall and weighing over 240 pounds, took over command of the company.

Monitoring the radio networks, Lieutenant Colonel Marcus J. Gravel, the commanding officer of the 1st Battalion, 1st Marines, decided to mount a rescue effort with his command group and the attached Company G, 2d Battalion, 5th Marines. Like Captain Batcheller, he had very little knowledge about the strength and disposition of the enemy forces in Hue. Indeed, he knew little about his own command, having met the Company G commander, Captain Charles L. Meadows, only that day.

Taking the same route as Company A, Gravel's relief expedition encountered only sporadic resistance until it crossed the An Cuu bridge. Upon reaching Batcheller's position about noon, Gravel realized that he had few options and that he had limited maneuverability with two rifle companies, a "ragtag . . . handful of tanks and people you've never seen before."

Gravel quickly saw that the trucks would be of little use in the narrow streets and ordered the men to dismount. The wounded, including Captain Batcheller, were put on the trucks and then sent back to Phu Bai which, Gravel later admitted "Was a terrible long shot." Although a gamble, Gravel believed it was the only way he was going to save the wounded. "We weren't going to get any helicopters in there . . . so we took them back." While not providing any escort, Gravel armed those wounded who could still fire weapons to provide what protection they could. The trucks completed the return trip to Phu Bai without incident.

With Lieutenant Colonel LaMontagne's tanks in the vanguard, the two Marine companies and the 1st Battalion, 1st Marines command group fought their way toward the MACV compound. As they passed through the gate to the cheers of the defenders, the cigar-chomping LaMontagne asked for help with the wounded. Some MACV advisors

then commandeered a vehicle to bring in the more badly injured Marines. At the same time, Gravel pushed Company G forward through the battered ranks of Company A. By 1530 hours, Gravel and his entire force was inside the compound.

Gravel reported to Army Colonel George O. Adkisson, the chief US advisor to the 1st ARVN Division and in command of the MACV compound. The two men failed to reach a rapport. According to Gravel, Adkisson had a plentiful supply of ammunition, weapons, and equipment that "he wasn't too willing to part with until he saw that if he wanted to keep his hat and ass together, he'd better be nice to us because we were all that he had."

Shortly after the 1st Battalion arrived at the MACV compound, General LaHue radioed Gravel to cross the river and relieve General Truong's headquarters in the Citadel. Captain Meadows remembered the orders were something to the effect "go up to the 1st ARVN Division headquarters and escort the CG (commanding general) back down to Phu Bai."

EARLY CASUALTIES: Two civilians of the Military Assistance Command, Vietnam, (MACV) help carry wounded Marines to the safety of the MACV compound during the early stages of the street fighting.

Gravel and his command group together with Meadow's Company G headed for the Route 1 bridge, spanning the Perfume River. The battalion commander had decided against taking the American tanks because he was not sure that the bridge could hold the weight of the M-48s and besides "they weren't terribly anxious to go, either." He collected a group of lighter ARVN tanks that he believed could navigate that bridge, "but they weren't interested." Keeping both the American and South Vietnamese tanks on the southern side of the river, Gravel decided to use them as direct support weapons for the infantry company.

Under cover of the tank and automatic weapons fire, Company G finally secured the bridge after taking out a machine gun position on the northern end. After the two lead platoons had crossed the river, they turned left and encountered "intense, absolutely intense fire" from almost every building in sight. With the setting sun in their eyes, the Marine infantry were at a distinct disadvantage, being both outgunned and outnumbered. Gravel realized "that we were no match for what was going on," and ordered a withdrawal.

The return to the southern bank was almost as difficult as the advance into the Citadel. Captain Meadows remembered that "I had 49 casualties the first day. . . . And almost every one of those was going across that one bridge and then getting back across that bridge." Gravel radioed Adkisson at the MACV compound for vehicles and men to assist in the recovery of the wounded and dead. After waiting for a time with no trucks showing up, Gravel walked across the bridge with his radio operator and interpreter "to find out where in the hell the vehicles were."

With additional men and transport, Gravel returned to the bridge. By this time, the Marines of Company G had commandeered some abandoned private automobiles and were loading the casualties on board. By the time they returned to the MACV compound, the Marines had given up on the idea of storming the Citadel.

In the Citadel itself, General Truong held on to the division headquarters and ordered ARVN units into the city. The relief force ordered by Trung on the 31st, the ARVN 7th Airborne Battalion and the

War weary —A radioman with Co G, 2d Bn, 5th Marines, pauses during their advance. Men from Co G linked up with Co A, 1st Bn, 1st Marines, for the breakthrough to the MACV compound.

3d Troop, 7th Armored Cavalry, departed their base area in the "Street Without Joy" sector of Thua Thien province for the 17-kilometer road trip south to Hue. About 0930 hours that morning, two North Vietnamese battalions intercepted and halted the relief force about 400 meters north of the Citadel. Only when reinforced by the 2d Airborne Battalion did the embattled ARVN column finally make it through the enemy lines. Moving along the northern wall of the Citadel, the relief force entered the northern gate into the 1st ARVN Division compound. In the heavy fighting, the South Vietnamese sustained 40 killed and 91 wounded, but claimed to have killed 270 of the enemy. The NVA destroyed four of the 12 ARVN cavalry troop armored personnel carriers.

Other ARVN units attempting to relieve the Citadel had even less success than the armored column from the north. The 2d and 3d Battalions from the 3d ARVN Regiment advanced along the northern bank of the Perfume River, but North Vietnamese defenders prevented them from entering the Citadel. Forced to fall back, the two battalions established positions outside the southeast wall of the city. The other two battalions of the regiment encountered strong NVA forces southwest of Hue. The 1st Battalion fought its way to the coast near Ba Lang with only three clips of ammunition left per man. South Vietnamese motorized junks landed the battalion near the northern gate the next day. The 4th Battalion remained engaged for several days with North Vietnamese units before being able to break free.

Despite the heavy combat in the city of Hue on 31 January, the American command still was unaware of the extent of the North Vietnamese effort in the city. General Westmoreland radioed back to Washington that night that the enemy had about three companies in the city. He observed that the Marines had sent a battalion to clean them out. As the Marines were soon to discover, it would take more than a battalion to reclaim Hue.

Gen. Vo Nguyen Giap —North Vietnam's Defense Minister and a master of surprise tactics, as the French had discovered nearly a quarter-century before Tet. The attack on Hue was bittersweet for him; among the buildings shelled was Quoc Hoc High School, which he had graduated from over 30 years earlier.

Wall-to-wall combat

7

The fight for southern Hue

THE REALITY of the situation soon became apparent to the Marines in Hue. The 1st ARVN Division was to take over responsibility for the fighting in the Citadel while the 1st Battalion, 1st Marines (1/1) was to clear the southern sector. On the morning of 1 February, Task Force X-Ray ordered Lieutenant Colonel Gravel to protect American citizens and facilities in the modern city and to secure the province headquarters and prison. Brigadier General LaHue, the Task Force X-Ray commander, like General Westmoreland, still underestimated the extent to which the enemy forces had penetrated the city. He told an impromptu press conference at Phu Bai that the US forces controlled the situation. In Hue, Lieutenant Colonel Gravel knew better.

At 0700 hours on the 1st, Gravel's battalion launched a two-company assault southwest of the MACV compound toward the prison and provincial headquarters about six blocks away. Although supported by tanks, the attack immediately stalled in the face of enemy B-40 rockets and automatic weapons fire from the windows of surrounding buildings. With the entire six blocks controlled by the NVA and Viet Cong forces, Gravel dissuaded Task Force X-Ray from attempting a tank-supported night attack against the objective.

Albeit frustrated in its attempt to advance to the south, the 1st Battalion, 1st Marines succeeded in expanding its defensive perimeter. The battalion occupied the University of Hue buildings across the

103

street from the MACV compound and used the open area bordering the river south of the Navy LCU ramp as an improvised landing zone.

Task Force X-Ray also began to realize that the situation in Hue was perhaps more serious than originally thought. Shortly after noon on the 1st, General LaHue called in Colonel Stanley S. Hughes, the commanding officer of the 1st Marines, and gave him tactical control of the Marine forces in the city. Hughes immediately relayed orders to Gravel that he was to conduct "sweep and clear operations in assigned area . . . to destroy enemy forces, protect US nationals, and restore that city (Hue) to US control."

Hughes also began to send reinforcements into the beleaguered city. Marine twin-rotor CH-46 Sea Knight helicopters brought Captain Michael P. Downs' Company F 2d Battalion, 5th Marines (2/5) into the landing zone below the LCU Ramp.

Downs, who was attached to Gravel's command, soon became aware of how little appreciation higher headquarters had of the situation confronting the Marines. Before he left, he had been told that his mission would be to protect the small groups of Americans isolated in the city. His company spent its first day in Hue trying to reach the Armed Forces Radio Station but never made it.

Fire support —In the street fighting for southern Hue, a Marine tank crew member mans the .50 cal. machine gun of his M-48 tank. The commander has positioned the tank behind a hastily built fortification for protection from enemy rockets.

The following morning, Gravel's battalion renewed its attack toward the provincial headquarters and prison, with only limited success. In heavy fighting, the Marines finally secured the local Armed Forces Radio Station and rescued the Americans there. The An Cuu bridge over the Phu Cam canal remained standing and the resupply route to Phu Bai stayed open.

The Marines continued to bring in supplies and reinforcements over Route 1 from Phu Bai through "Rough Rider" armed truck convoys. On the afternoon of the 2 February, Company H, 2/5 Marines, commanded by Captain G. Ronald Christmas, arrived by Rough Rider to join the fight for the city. Accompanied by Army dusters and two Ontos, small tracked antitank vehicles, the truck convoy encountered resistance about 300 meters from the MACV compound as the enemy opened up with a heavy fusillade of .50 caliber and small arms fire. The Army dusters with their quad .50 machine

GENTLY DOES IT: In action near the University of Hue, Marines from Co A, 1st Bn, 1st Marines, lower a wounded comrade to the ground. The capture of the University was one of the first successes of the Marine forces in their counteroffensive against the Communist units that had occupied most of the city.

guns and the Ontos, each with their six mounted 106mm recoilless rifles, quickly suppressed the enemy weapons. While the enemy rockets disabled one truck, the Marines successfully towed the vehicle to safety. Two French photographers, Cathy Leroy and Francois Mazure, took refuge with the convoy after being released by North Vietnamese soldiers.

At Da Nang, General Cushman, the III MAF commander, discussed the situation with General Lam, the South Vietnamese commander. At first, the allies had not wanted to use air support and heavy caliber artillery because of the cultural significance of Hue to the Vietnamese. Cushman declared that he wasn't about to "open up on the old

palace and all the historical buildings in there," and
that Lam would have to make that decision. The two
commanders agreed to lift some of the artillery re-
strictions. Cushman ordered a brigade from the 1st
Cavalry Division (Airmobile) to land west of the city
and attempt to block the enemy lines of
communication in that direction.

At Phu Bai, on 2 February, Colonel Robert D.
Bohn, the 5th Marines commander, conferred with
Lieutenant Colonel Ernest C. Cheatham, the
commander of the 2/5 Marines. Cheatham
remembered Bohn telling him to "saddle up what
you need out of H&S (Headquarters and Support)
Company" and that he and his command group was
going to accompany the 1st Marines headquarters,

Wall-to-wall combat

MOVE!
Under the protective cover of the 90mm gun of an M-48 tank, Marine infantry rush across a street in the initial fighting for Hue city. The Marines soon discovered that employing tanks in southern Hue offered only limited protection.

commanded by Colonel Hughes, into Hue the following day.

The following morning, the command groups of both the 1st Marines and the 2/5 Marines left Phu Bai for Hue in a Rough Rider convoy. The weather had deteriorated—it had turned cold for Vietnam, temperature about 50 degrees, and damp, nearly a constant fog, mist, or rain. Like similar convoys, the two headquarters ran the gauntlet of enemy B-40 rockets and machine gun fire once they crossed the bridge into Hue. One rocket took out one of the Ontos that was running shotgun. Despite the enemy ambuscade, Colonel Hughes established his command post in the MACV command post by 1300 hours that afternoon.

A veteran commander and holder of the Navy Cross for action on Cape Gloucester in World War II, Colonel Hughes held a hasty council of war. He returned the three 2d Battalion companies under the operational control of Lieutenant Colonel Gravel to Lieutenant Colonel Cheatham. Gravel retained command of his Company A. Hughes assigned Gravel the mission of keeping open the main supply route while Cheatham took over the main attack towards the provincial headquarters and prison.

Cheatham recalled that Colonel Hughes turned to him and said: "I want you to move up to the Hue University building, and your right flank is the Perfume River and you're going to have an exposed left flank. I want you to attack through the city and clean the NVA out." Cheatham remembered that he just stood there and waited for the colonel to continue with his orders. Hughes then abruptly remarked: "If you're looking for any more, you aren't going to get it. Move out!" As Cheatham started for the door, Colonel Hughes told Cheatham softly "You do it any way you want to and you get any heat from above, I'll take care of that."

After establishing himself in his new command post at the university, Cheatham soon discovered that he had no magic formula. Directly across the street from the university were two large buildings, the province treasury building and the post office, occupied by North Vietnamese troops blocking any further Marine advance. Marine bullets and LAWs hardly made a dent on the 4-5-foot-thick walls of the treasury building. Cheatham's troops attacked the two buildings about six times and were repulsed each time over a period of nearly 18 hours.

As Captain Christmas, the Company H commander, explained, the Marines just did not have enough troops. One company could maintain a frontage of about one city block. With only three companies under his command, Cheatham had two companies forward and held one back in reserve. This left the left flank open, exposed to enemy machine gun positions.

On the morning of the 4th, Colonel Hughes discussed the situation with both of his battalion commanders. In light of his previous experience, Lieutenant Colonel Gravel was not surprised that the 2/5 Marines had not made any further progress.

Any cover will do—Early in the fighting for southern Hue, a Marine crouches behind a concrete pole in the face of enemy sniper fire.

THE HOLE PUNCHER: Marines from Co H, 2d Bn, 5th Marines, haul 3.5-inch rocket rounds up to the roof of one of the buildings of Hue University. The Marines discovered early in the fighting that the 3.5-inch rocket was an effective weapon in house-to-house combat, providing enough punch to blast through masonry and walls.

He believed "that there perhaps was some second guessing down at headquarters on the inability of 1/1 to attack." Although not wishing Cheatham any misfortune, he now felt somewhat vindicated. Colonel Hughes decided to place Gravel's unit on the 2d Battalion's exposed flank and continue the assault.

At 0700 hours, the companies of the 2d Battalion renewed the attack. Learning from the previous day's fighting, the Marines soon adapted to the city street fighting so different from the paddy and jungle war in the countryside. Christmas's company, blasting its way through walls and courtyards with 3.5-inch rockets and squad and fireteam rushes, captured the public health building. From there,

WINDOW ON THE WAR: From the vantage of a Hue University classroom window a Marine rifleman fires his M-16 semiautomatic rifle at Communist troops lodged in buildings across the street. Other Marines watch, one even leaving his rifle—almost carelessly, or so it seems—on the window ledge.

they could support by fire Down's company's attempt to take the treasury building.

According to Captain Christmas, the Marines found a new use for the 106mm recoilless rifle. The Marines employed smoke grenades to cover their movements, but the NVA used this as a signal: "Everything that was on our flank just opened up on that street." To counter the enemy tactic, the Marines would "pop smoke," determine the general location of the enemy machine gun, and then "here would come a mule-mounted 106 (the mechanical mule was a small flatbed four-wheeled vehicle often used to ferry about a 106mm recoilless rifle). . . ." The crew "would wheel that thing out. Go through the full drill . . . crank off" the .50 caliber aiming round, and then pull the lanyard to fire the 106mm round. With the backblast of the recoilless rifle creating a cloud of dust and the 106mm round forcing the enemy to keep his head down, the infantrymen would seize the opportunity to cross the street.

In his assault on the treasury building, Captain Downs also used the 106mm recoilless rifle to his advantage. With its thick walls and large steel door, the treasury building remained impervious to the Marine infantry company's repeated efforts to force its way inside. Lieutenant Colonel Cheatham then suggested that they dismount one of the 106s from its mechanical mule, carry it up to the second floor of one of the university buildings, where they would have a direct line of sight at this formidable door. Cheatham directed the crew to place the gun in a corner window. They fired a round from the .50 caliber gun mounted on the tube and then attached a long leading line to the firing mechanism. As the other Marines vacated the building, the gunner pulled the string. The resulting backblast caved in half the building, burying the weapon, but the round knocked open the door.

The NVA still were in force inside the treasury building and managed to cover with fire all avenues of approach. Cheatham's executive officer, Major Ralph J. Salvati, came up with an idea to employ the E-8 CS (tear gas) launcher. Light and portable, the launcher could fire 16 CS canisters in four volleys and produce in minutes a large chemical cloud. He told Cheatham that he had seen a stack of the launchers in the MACV compound and suggested that he go back and get them. Cheatham agreed and Salvati commandeered a jeep and driver, drove back to the compound for the launchers before

YARD TO YARD: In fighting in one of the upper-class residential sections of southern Hue, two Marines of Co H, 2d Bn, 5th Marines, rush through a well-kept yard. Progress was slow, companies advancing a house at a time.

rejoining Captain Downs in a wrecked school building adjoining the treasury. Donning gas masks, Salvati and two Marines rushed into the courtyard, aimed one of the launchers, and then took cover behind a wall. He pulled the lanyard, but the launcher failed to fire. Salvati then found a power-cell battery and wired it to the firing mechanism. This time the E-8 launcher hurled the CS canisters into the treasury compound.

With the gas seeping into the Treasury building and under a barrage of 81mm mortar and 3.5-inch rocket covering fire, Company F Marines, wearing gas masks, launched their attack. Most of the enemy troops broke and fled the building.

On the 2d Battalion's left flank, Lieutenant Colonel Gravel began clearing his objective area. He had only one infantry company, Company A, now commanded by First Lieutenant Ray L. Smith, who took over from the wounded Captain Batcheller. Gravel's first objective was the Joan of Arc School and Church, only about 100 yards from the MACV compound. The NVA put up a fierce resistance. In the convent the Marines fought, said Gravel, "wall to wall, room to room." A Marine would place a C-4 explosive plastic against a wall, stand back, and then a fire team or squad would rush through the gaping hole.

Forward search —A Marine carrying an M-16 rifle, a cigarette almost nonchalantly dangling from his lips, climbs through a wall into a courtyard in search of NVA and VC troops.

The Marines captured one wing of the school. Sergeant Alfred Gonzalez led troops from the 3d Platoon into one room where they came under direct B-40 fire from a window across the courtyard. Gonzalez rushed forward and fired about 10 LAW rockets and silenced the enemy. Suddenly the room erupted in smoke and fire. One last B-40 rocket smashed through a grilled window and struck Sergeant Gonzalez directly in the midsection, killing him instantly. Gonzalez was awarded the Medal of Honor posthumously for an earlier action during the ambush of Company A on 31 January.

The Marine company turned its attention to the church, which sat beside the school complex among some trees and residential structures. According to Lieutenant Gravel, "it was just a beautiful, beautiful church." As the lead platoon rushed the church, enemy troops waiting in the rafters threw down grenades, killing or wounding several of the Marines. Left with little choice, Gravel gave the

BACKBLAST:
Two Marines keep their ears covered after firing their jeep-mounted 106mm recoilless rifle. The 106mm round served a dual purpose; it forced the enemy to keep his head down, while at the same its backblast created a dust cloud that provided cover for infantrymen to rush across the street.

order to destroy the church. Marine 81mm mortars, 106mm recoilless rifle, and automatic weapons fire reduced it rubble.

On the 4th, more reinforcements and supplies continued to arrive by truck convoy over Route 1, but they were to be the last to take that route for several days. Company B, 1/1 Marines arrived by Rough Rider from Phu Bai, providing Lieutenant Colonel Gravel with two companies to wage his fight in Hue. That evening, however, NVA sappers blew up the bridge over the Phu Cam canal, closing the land route to the city. The only means of resupply remaining was by ship or by helicopter. With the continuous low overcast, flying conditions were marginal at best. The ship channel up the Perfume

River from the sea was relatively narrow and subject to enemy shore bombardment or automatic weapons fire.

For the time being, however, the 1st Marines had received replenishment of men, food, and ammunition. A truck convoy on 3 February brought enough food rations to sustain the two battalions for two days. An LCU docked at the LCU Ramp on the 5th with additional rations, sufficient to last for more than 10 days. Although the Marines expended ammunition at more than 10 times the normal rate, the 1st Marines experienced no major shortages. The supply of gas masks, however, occasionally ran low.

Lieutenant Colonels Gravel and Cheatham both complained about the lack of adequate maps. The only maps that they brought with them were the

standard tactical ones, which provided little detail of the city streets and buildings. Eventually all of the battalions obtained basic tourist maps of Hue, which numbered the prominent sites and buildings. The Marines used the numbers to coordinate their movements.

Prior to having the tourist maps, Marine commanders had used the color of buildings to designate their locations. Captain Christmas recalled some of the confusion that they had with the color scheme. He would get on the radio and declare "I'm in a pink building." Captain Downs would acknowledge and state he was in the "green building." Meadows would then affirm that he was in the "brown building." At that point, Lieutenant Colonel Cheatham, who was monitoring the radio

SMOKE THEM OUT:
A squad of Marines wearing gas masks, prepares to flush out NVA troops entrenched in fixed positions. The selective use of CS gas proved effective against the NVA in enclosed surroundings.

Wall-to-wall combat

NO SANCTUARY:
A Marine from Co A, 1st Bn, 1st Marines, searches for enemy troops in front of a church altar. Both Christian churches and Buddhist pagodas sustained heavy damage as the enemy often used them for defensive positions.

network, "would come up and say, "where the hell are the green, brown, and pink buildings?'"

On the morning of 5 February, both battalions renewed the offensive. Captain Christmas's Company H anchored the right flank as it pushed forward on Le Loi Street close to the river front. On the left flank, Lieutenant Colonel Gravel attempted to maintain a two-block front, "which is simple enough. But when you realize that there's no one on your left in these other blocks, you've got to expand this out." This required troops of which the battalion commander had too few.

Cheatham's battalion on the right made faster progress, but also ran into heavy resistance. The

battalion had an operating area of about 11 blocks wide and eight to nine blocks deep. As Cheatham stated: "It wasn't that big," although "it looked plenty big at the time." With little room to maneuver, the Marines had to take one building at a time. The battalion would "pick a point and attempt to break that one strongpoint," and then work from there. Lieutenant Colonel Cheatham observed that the enemy "defended on every other street. . . . When we would take him off one street, we would usually push through the next row of houses fairly quickly and then hit another defensive position."

Although supported by four to five tanks, the

Enemy church captured —Marines from Co A, 1st Bn, 1st Marines, on the steps of a church shortly after they had captured it in heavy fighting. The war in Hue knew no sentiment and recognized few sanctuaries.

Marines found the lighter and more mobile Ontos, the 106mm recoilless rifles, the 3.5 inch rockets, CS launchers, and mortars more adaptable to their use. According to Cheatham, "The moment a tank stuck its nose around the corner of a building, it looked like the Fourth of July. . . ." The tank immediately became the target of all of the enemy weapons from B-40 antitank rounds to automatic weapons fire. Cheatham recalled one tank that was hit 121 times and that another went through five or six crews. Tankers who survived came out of their vehicles looking "like they were punch drunk."

Cheatham called the Ontos with its six 106mm recoilless rifles as "big a help as any item of gear that we had that was not organic to the battalion." He would employ the vehicle in hull defilade, "even if the defilade was only behind a brick wall" since the Ontos was vulnerable to enemy rocket fire. The battalion commander also liked the 3.5-inch rockets that provided him with the penetrating power to punch holes into thick-walled buildings as well as support the riflemen.

With the fighting at close range, both battalions made little use in the first days of the advance of supporting arms. The low-lying cloud cover made close air support impracticable. Neither unit used heavy artillery until the fifth or sixth day of the battle and then largely for interdiction of enemy escape routes. As Lieutenant Colonel Gravel explained, they could not observe the results of a mission well enough: "You lose the rounds in the buildings, in the streets, and you don't know where, and you have a difficult time with perspective."

The Marine battalions' own mortars took up the supporting role slack. Captain Downs regularly employed 81mm mortars within 35 meters of his position: "We were on one side of the street and 81's were fired on the other side of the street." Lieutenant Colonel Cheatham used his mortars "just like a hammer on top of a building. And if you put enough 81 rounds on top of a building, pretty soon the roof falls in. And this is simply what we did with it."

In their slow methodical advance, both battalions took casualties but inflicted heavier ones on the North Vietnamese defenders. By 6 February, the 2/5 Marines had reached the provincial headquarters.

Wall-to-wall combat

HOME FRONT:
In the struggle to recover southern Hue a Marine fires a burst from his M-60 machine gun out of the bathroom window of a house.

119

The hospital, the Cercle Sportif, and the Hue University Library were all in Marine hands. Lieutenant Colonel Cheatham assigned Captain Christmas's Company H to take the province capital building. Under cover of mortars, machine guns, tank fire, and a cloud of CS gas, Company H, wearing gas masks, rushed the building. The North Vietnamese soldiers fought back valiantly, but as the CS permeated the building their resistance slackened. By 1430 hours, the company had secured the building and Gunnery Sergeant Frank A. Thomas ripped down the Viet Cong flag waving from the building's flagpole. To both Americans and Vietnamese, the removal of the enemy banner symbolized that the tide of battle had turned.

According to South Vietnamese law and American military practice in Vietnam, the US flag was to be flown only when accompanied by the Republic of Vietnam's national ensign. Before the attack, Captain Christmas discussed the possibility of flying the American colors from the province headquarters flagpole. Despite the prohibition, Cheatham gave Christmas permission to display the US flag without the South Vietnamese. About 1600 hours that afternoon, Sergeant Thomas and two other Marines in front of CBS television cameras raised the Stars and Strips, causing a minor furor at more senior headquarters. The company removed the flag when they departed the provincial compound.

Refugees —Homeless from the fighting in their city, two Vietnamese women wash their clothes and collect cooking and drinking water from the Perfume River.

It had, nevertheless, been a good day for the 2/5 Marines. Company F had taken its objective and Company G, also in hard fighting, had captured the province prison.

The following morning the two Marine battalions renewed their offensive. Much to their surprise, both units made relatively rapid progress, encountering only sporadic enemy resistance. With the capture of the provincial headquarters, apparently the site of the command post of the 4th NVA Regiment, much of the enemy morale in southern Hue collapsed. As Lieutenant Colonel Gravel later related, the enemy appeared to "lose his stomach . . . for the fight." The main force units, according to Gravel, "sort of evaporated . . . and he left some local force—rinky dinks . . . when his defense crumbled, it crumbled."

The enemy, nevertheless, had the ability to make things uncomfortable for the Marines. Snipers continued to fire at the Marines and occasionally the NVA would make a last ditch stand for a particular structure. Intermittent mortar and rocket attacks continued to take their toll of Marines and South Vietnamese civilians. On the morning of 7 February Communist sappers blew up the bridge across the Perfume River connecting southern Hue with the Citadel. While the Marines watched, the center span fell into the water. Hue was now indeed two cities.

By 10 February, despite isolated pockets of enemy troops continuing to fight, the two battalions had reached their final objectives and the Marine command declared southern Hue secure. Assisted by US military and civilian advisors, the South Vietnamese authorities established a refugee center at the University for the thousands of homeless civilians caught in the conflict. The National Police started to restore some semblance of civil order and

SAFE PASSAGE: A Marine from Co H, 2d Bn, 5th Marines, carries a struggling woman patient from the Hue hospital to safety. The Marine battalion recaptured the hospital from the Communists after several days of hard fighting.

Wall-to-wall combat

FLIGHT AND FIGHT: Refugees retreating from the fighting pass a Marine tank going in the opposite direction toward the battle. The Americans established a refugee center for the Vietnamese homeless in the University grounds.

Wall-to-wall combat

Marines carry a wounded comrade in a poncho back to the 2d Bn, 5th Marines, aid station for medical treatment. During the battle for Hue, the Marines lost 142 dead and 857 seriously wounded. ARVN losses were 357 killed and 1,830 wounded. Allied forces claimed 4,421 enemy killed and 45 prisoners.

began to take harsh measures against the wholesale looting that occurred in the wake of the Marine advance by both ARVN soldiers and civilians.

By the 13th, Marine engineers had replaced the An Cuu bridge over the Phu Cam canal and reinforcements and supplies in truck convoys flowed into the divided city. While Lieutenant Colonel

Gravel's 1st Battalion, 1st Marines protected the bridge and continued mopping up in the city, Cheatham's battalion entered a new area of operations south of the city. The struggle for Hue City south of the Perfume River was largely over. But the battle for the Citadel had only just begun.

Taking the tower

AFTER ENJOYING some initial success, the South Vietnamese Army's offensive in the Citadel had come to a standstill. On 1 February, ARVN units retook the Tay Loc airfield from the North Vietnamese. Then on 4 February the 1st Battalion, 3d ARVN Regiment then captured the An Hoa gate on the northwest wall and then attacked towards the western corner of the Citadel. On the following day, the 4th Battalion, 2d ARVN Regiment continued the push, advancing all the way to the southwest wall. At this juncture, the North Vietnamese counterattacked. Using grappling hooks, on the night of 6-7 February the NVA drove the ARVN battalion off the wall, forcing it back to the airfield.

In the meantime, the Airborne Task Force, which earlier had relieved the 4th Battalion on the northeast wall, had made some progress in its sector. Its advance, however, by the end of the first week had also come to a halt.

During this period, General Truong, the 1st ARVN Division commander, had brought additional units into the fighting for the Citadel. By 7 February, Truong had in the Citadel four Airborne battalions, the Black Panther Company, two armored cavalry squadrons, the 3d ARVN Infantry Regiment, and a battalion from the 2d ARVN Regiment and a company from the 1st ARVN Regiment.

Despite these reinforcements, his troops were not making any headway against the NVA. For the next few days, the ARVN ran up against well-entrenched NVA troops who prevented any further advance. The North Vietnamese still controlled about 60 percent of the Citadel and continued to receive replacements and supplies.

Taking the tower

REINFORCING THE FRONTLINE: ARVN soldiers accompanied by Australian advisors board a Marine CH-53A, a heavy twin-engine single-rotor transport helicopter, to reinforce the embattled ARVN 1st Division headquarters compound in the old Citadel sector of Hue.

To the west, the 3d Brigade of the US 1st Air Cavalry Division (Airmobile) had difficulty in severing the enemy infiltration and supply routes into the Citadel. Lifted into a landing zone about 10 kilometers northwest of Hue, the brigade advanced south and east towards Hue. After a forced night march on 4 February, the 2d Battalion, 12th Cavalry reached high ground overlooking Hue. Exhausted and overextended, the battalion was in no position to close with the NVA and halt the nightly flow of enemy supplies into the Citadel. As one 1st Cavalry soldier remarked, "We had gotten less than six hours sleep in the past 48 hours. We didn't have any water and the river water was too muddy to drink."

The 5th Battalion, 7th Cavalry tried to link up

with the 2d Battalion, but on 7 February ran into
an NVA force that had infiltrated between the two
American units. Forced to leave its high ground on
9 February, the 2d Battalion attacked north toward
the 5th Battalion. Passing through the lines of the
latter unit, the 2d Battalion troopers struck the
entrenched enemy in the town of Thong Bon Tre.
In a daylong battle the two battalions cleared the
village. But the enemy supply lines remained open.

With the South Vietnamese stalemated in their
efforts to clear the Citadel, General Truong, on 9
February, decided to ask for American assistance.
General Cushman agreed.

General LaHue, the Task Force X-Ray
commander, called on the 1st Battalion, 5th Marines

(1/5). A battalion of the US Army 1st Brigade, 101st Airborne Division, recently arrived at Phu Bai, relieved the Marine battalion. On 10 February, Company A of the 1st Battalion accompanied a Rough Rider convoy from Phu Bai to Hue. At the An Cuu bridge, the convoy halted. Marine engineers, discovered that the bridge had been too badly damaged to repair. While the engineers and trucks returned to Phu Bai, the infantry dismounted and made their way by foot over the broken span. The company reported to the 1st Marines at the MACV compound.

At Phu Bai, Major Robert H. Thompson, who had just taken over command of the 1st Battalion, discussed the plans for the insertion of the battalion into the Citadel with General LaHue. The Task Force X-Ray commander told Thompson that they had little intelligence on the situation in Hue, only that the South Vietnamese needed help.

The Marine command prepared to coordinate supporting arms fire into the Citadel area. On the morning of the 10th, Colonel John F. Barr, the commander of the Marine artillery at Phu Bai asked one of his junior staff officers, First Lieutenant Alexander W. Wells, Jr., to report to him. Barr informed Wells that he had volunteered the young lieutenant to establish a forward fire direction center in the Citadel as American forces were entering the battle for the old city. Lieutenant Wells, whose tour of duty in Vietnam was about over, was not overly anxious to take on the new assignment, but Colonel Barr gave him little choice. The mission was to be for only 24 hours.

About 1630 hours that afternoon, a Marine helicopter flew Wells and his radio operator from Phu Bai to the ARVN 1st Division Headquarters. Leaping out from the hovering aircraft, the two Marines took refuge in a nearby Quonset hut which served as a temporary command post for allied advisors to the Black Panther company. Wells remembered the hut as "full of Australians playing cards and drinking scotch." Reaching the 1st Division Headquarters, Wells received a briefing from General Truong and his staff.

After midnight, two ARVN soldiers, whom Wells believed to be Rangers, led the two Americans through assorted back alleys and side streets to their

Head down —Marine infantrymen of the 1st Bn, 5th Marines, take cover from heavy enemy automatic fire in the battle for the Citadel.

CROSSING THE PERFUME RIVER:
For the supply and movement of troops to both the Citadel and southern Hue, the US and South Vietnamese forces were very much dependent on landing craft and small river craft. Here Marine and naval riflemen on board a harbor utility craft, YFU-72, watch for enemy snipers hidden in positions along the shore or ensconced in the walls of the Citadel.

unit. Holed up inside the ruins of a Buddhist pagoda, which Wells nicknamed the "Alamo," near the Imperial palace, the ARVN troops numbered less than 100 and were completely surrounded by the enemy. For the next 14 days, using his map and adjusting fires by sound, Wells called in Marine 8-inch and 155mm artillery fire and naval gunfire from two destroyers and a cruiser lying off the coast.

On the morning of 11 February, Marine CH-46 Sea Knight helicopters helilifted three platoons of Captain Fern Jennings' Company B, 1/5 Marines to the 1st ARVN Division headquarters compound. Wounded by enemy small arms fire as he approached the landing zone, the pilot of the CH-46 carrying the 3d Platoon veered off and returned to Phu Bai. That afternoon, Company A from the 1st Battalion and five tanks from the 1st Tank Battalion boarded an LCU at the ramp in the new city for the

cross river passage to the Citadel. By that evening, the reinforcements were also in the 1st Division compound.

In the meantime, Major Thompson together with his command group and the Company B 3d Platoon, arrived by Rough Rider at the 1st Marines CP in southern Hue. Reporting to Colonel Hughes, Thompson discussed with the regimental commander the situation in the old city. Thompson would take across the river the following day his command group, Company C, and the remaining platoon from Company B. Company D for the time

Taking the tower

FORWARD OBSERVER: A small US observation aircraft, used to call in artillery and naval gunfire and to direct air strikes, makes a low pass over Hue on 23 February. The damaged buildings in the background provide evidence of the severity and extent of the fighting.

being would be attached to the 2d Battalion, 5th Marines (2/5) in southern Hue.

Shortly after noon on the 12th, both Companies C and D arrived at the MACV compound in Hue. Company C then joined the 1st Battalion command group and the 3d Platoon of Company B at the LCU ramp, awaiting transport. Enemy gunfire from the walls of the Citadel and from both riverbanks delayed the Navy LCUs that were to carry the battalion. Finally in the late afternoon, the craft were able to get through and docked at the LCU ramp. Although the LCUs took fire from enemy

Taking the tower

A HIGH-RISK PROFESSION: An M-48 tank with a shield of Marine infantrymen from the 1st Bn, 5th Marines, advance flanked by the wall of the Citadel. Although the tanks sustained little damage, casualties among tank crews were high. In the course of one day's fighting, one tank had five different crews.

gunners while under way, the Marines landed without incident and made their way overland into the 1st Division compound.

Major Thompson met with General Truong and confirmed the battle plans for the following day. The 1st Battalion was to take over the former Airborne sector along the southeast wall. Complicating the situation was the non-arrival of a Vietnamese Marine task force from Saigon that was to relieve the battered airborne units. The Airborne units were already at the Phu Bai airfield ready to return to Saigon on the aircraft bringing in the Vietnamese

Marines. According to the plan, the Vietnamese Marines were to protect the 1st Battalion's right flank. Although not yet knowing the Vietnamese Marine area of operations, Thompson radioed Colonel Hughes, "Unless directed otherwise, intend to commence attack at 13 (February) 0800."

As planned, Thompson launched his assault the following morning with Company A in the lead. Fifteen minutes into the attack, the NVA from commanding positions in a tower off the northeastern wall opened up with B-40 rockets, fragmentation grenades, and automatic weapons.

The Marines responded with their M-16s. A recoilless rifle team and a lead tank reinforced the fires of the infantrymen. In less than 10 minutes, Company A sustained 35 casualties, including the company commander, Captain J. J. Browe.

Major Thompson ordered Company A back to regroup and directed First Lieutenant Scott A. Nelson, the commander of his reserve, Company C, to move up on the right flank of Company B to take over Company A's former sector. About 1300 hours, the battalion renewed the attack. With two tanks in the lead, Company B advanced about 300 meters before heavy enemy fire from the tower stopped the Marines once more. Although damaged by NVA rocket rounds, the tanks were still able to fire about 200 rounds of .50 caliber machine gun and four 90mm shells at the enemy position.

Into action —A Marine M-60 machine gun team from Co C, 1st Bn, 5th Marines, fires from behind a tree. The M-60's light, folding tripod made it easy for a gunner to quickly change his position to get a better angle of fire.

With the infantry and tanks unable to budge the enemy, Colonel Hughes radioed Major Thompson to hold his positions, "reorganize and prepare plans for continuing attack indicating type fire support deemed necessary and desirable." Thompson replied that he required the full spectrum of allied fire power to support his attack on the next day. He wanted to walk the "artillery in front of advancing troops." According to Thompson, he needed both 8-inch and 155mm artillery fire and close air support. That evening the battalion commander requested that his Company D be returned to him.

On the southern side of the city, Captain Myron C. Harrington, the Company D commander, brought two of his three platoons to the LCU Ramp for transport across the river. Two LCUs were at the wharf, but loaded with supplies. Harrington squeezed on board with his headquarters group and one squad. Although North Vietnamese gunners on the wall fired at the two craft, the LCUs made it safely across and deposited both the supplies and Harrington and his small group ashore.

The LCUs returned to the ramp for the remaining two platoons. Again, as the craft made their way to the northern landing site, NVA guns opened up. On the southern bank, two Marine 4.2-inch mortars responded, firing both high explosive and CS shells at the enemy positions on the Citadel wall. Suddenly the two LCUs turned around and returned to the ramp. The shifting wind had brought the CS into

the two boats, half blinding and choking both the troops and sailors. The LCU commanders decided against making a return trip.

On the opposite shore, a frustrated Captain Harrington feared that he might have to spend the night separated from the bulk of his company. Fortunately, about midnight, a Navy Swift boat with a mounted .50 caliber machine gun and towing three junks arrived at the LCU ramp. The Marines embarked on board the junks and tried again to reach the northern bank. Despite enemy gunfire the Swift boat safely towed the three junks to a point offshore where the Marines then rowed them to the wharf where Captain Harrington was impatiently waiting.

Once inside the Citadel on the 14th, the company went into reserve while the rest of the battalion continued the attack. Artillery and naval ships slammed shells into the Citadel and for the first time in over a week, the overcast lifted enough for Marine

BLOOPING A SNIPER:
A Marine grenadier from the 1st Bn, 5th Marines, fires his M-79 grenade launcher at an enemy sniper in the Citadel fighting. The single shot M-79, known as the "Bloop Tube" because of the sound it made, could hurl a 40mm grenade to an effective range of 350 meters.

fixed-wing F-4B Phantom and F-8 Crusader jets to fly close air support missions.

Despite the efforts of the artillery and the air strikes, the tower still stood and the Marine infantry attack remained stalled. Companies C and B bore the brunt of the assault with Company B on the left flank going against the tower. Advancing cautiously, the Marines destroyed an NVA rocket position and captured one enemy soldier who walked up to them. Yet at the end of the day. the battalion had only gained 100 yards before pulling back to night defensive positions. The following day, it would be Harrington's company's turn to go against the tower.

On the 15th, artillery and naval gunfire once more bombarded the Citadel wall. This time under

the pounding, part of the tower gave way. Then two F-4B Phantoms streaked in low under the gray overcast and dropped 250- and 500-pound bombs. The tower crumbled even further. Supported by tanks and Ontos, Harrington's troops rushed forward with Company C on its right flank. The North Vietnamese fought back stubbornly and Major Thompson sent one of his reserve companies, Company B, to reinforce the two lead companies. After six hours of fierce fighting, including hand-to-hand combat, Captain Harrington's Company D finally drove the remaining NVA out of the ruins of the tower. The struggle for the tower had cost both sides dearly. The Marines lost six men killed and over 50 wounded. They killed over 20 of the enemy.

Through the night and into the early hours of

MOVING IN:
Using scattered furniture and buildings for cover, Marines of Co L, 3d Bn, 5th Marines, advance upon enemy positions in the Citadel. On 21 February Co L reinforced the 1st Bn, 5th Marines, in the old city.

Taking
the tower

SEAT OF VICTORY:
A Marine
holding his
weapon aloft
sits victoriously
on the throne of
the former
Vietnamese
emperors in the
ancient imperial
palace in the
Citadel. The
palace had been
recaptured by
Vietnamese
Marines on 24
February.

15-16 February the NVA tried to retake the tower,
but Harrington's men successfully defended their
hard-won gains. On the following morning, Major
Thompson continued the battalion's advance
southeast along the wall. The Marines immediately
made contact, "engaging the enemy at extremely
close range." Despite the determined NVA
resistance, the Marines made some headway,
fighting from house to house and from street to
street. In the daylong fighting, the Marines killed
another 63 North Vietnamese while suffering losses
of 7 killed and 47 wounded.

For the next few days, the 1st Battalion Marines
encountered the same close quarter combat. In

contrast to the Communist units in southern Hue, the Marines found that the enemy in the Citadel used "better city-fighting tactics, improved the already formidable defenses, dug trenches, built roadblocks and conducted counterattacks to regain redoubts which were important to his defensive scheme." Moreover the narrow streets in the Citadel together with the strong stone structures in the older city reinforced the enemy defenses.

The battalion countered the enemy fixed defenses with heavy artillery, naval gunfire, and fixed-wing airstrikes when the weather permitted, as well as liberal use of riot control agents. Major Thompson placed his attached tanks and Ontos under the control of the tank platoon commander. Using the infantry to lay down a base of fire and to provide a screen, the Marines employed both the mobile Ontos and the platoon of tanks for direct fire support. At first, the M-48 tanks' 90mm guns were relatively ineffective against the concrete and stone houses; shells even ricocheted back onto the Americans. The tankers then started to use concrete piercing fused shells which "resulted in excellent penetration and walls were breached with two to four rounds." Although casualties among the crews were high, the tanks themselves withstood direct hits by the enemy B-40 rockets with relatively little damage.

From firing positions on the southern bank of the Perfume River, the Marine 4.2-inch mortar detachment supported the battalion's attack with both high explosive and CS rounds. The 4.2 CS shells proved more effective than the E-8 Dispensers in the built-up area in the Citadel. They penetrated the tile roofs of the buildings and "concentrated the full power of the round in the building rather than relying on the infiltration of the CS gas from outside." Enemy prisoners testified to the demoralizing effect of the gas on their units, although some NVA officers and senior NCOs carried gas masks with them into battle.

As the Marine battalion painfully inched forward, the enemy forces within the Citadel were having their own problems. On the night of the 16th, the ARVN unit at the "Alamo" with Lieutenant Wells intercepted a North Vietnamese radio message ordering a battalion-sized reinforcement through the west gate. Lieutenant Wells then called artillery and naval gunfire missions on the gate and on a nearby bridge across the moat. According to Wells, the 155mm battery at Phu Bai and the 5-inch guns from a destroyer responded to the mission within three minutes and continued firing for over ten minutes. Wells remembered, "there was screaming on the enemy radio—they had received a direct hit on the moat bridge killing their general. . . ." The general apparently was the commander of the forces within the Citadel. About midnight, his successor radioed to his superiors the news of the death of the previous commander and recommended that he be allowed to withdraw his forces from the city. The higher headquarters denied this request and told the new

Street machine —A Marine from the 1st Bn, 5th Marines, rests in an abandoned pedicab after helping to secure a street in the old city of Hue. A common form of street transport in Vietnam, the carriage was pulled by a bicycle, earning it the name pedicab.

SINGLE FILE:
A patrol from Co A, 1st Bn, 1st Marines, crosses a small battle-scarred bridge in the company's new operating area south of the Perfume River.

commanding officer "to remain in position and fight."

Although the NVA in the Citadel were now fighting a rearguard action, they contested nearly every piece of ground. The South Vietnamese Marines had advanced only 400 meters in two days in the western sector of the old city. Even with their mounting casualties, the enemy command continued to throw replacements into the fight and their supply lines remained open.

FIRST AID:
—A Navy
corpsman
bandages a
wounded Marine
from Co H, 2d
Bn, 5th Marines.
Navy doctors,
nurses and Navy
enlisted
corpsmen
provides
medical support
to the Marines.

At Phu Bai on 17 February, General West-moreland held a council of war at the newly established MACV Forward headquarters under General Abrams. At the conference, the American commanders decided to reinforce the 3d Brigade of the 1st Air Cavalry with another battalion from the division and another from the 101st Airborne Brigade. They also promised to make available two battalions from the 101st to Task Force X-Ray to reinforce the Marines southwest of Hue.

The allied plans called for the 1st Cavalry to press the NVA from the northwest while the two 101st battalions with Task Force X-Ray were to block enemy avenues of escape to the south and southwest. Outside of the Citadel, 1/1 Marines and 2/5 Marines were to continue to clear the modern city and expand operations to the south and east of Hue.

In the Citadel, General Truong, the ARVN 1st Division commander, prepared for the final thrust against an entrenched and determined enemy. He assigned the Vietnamese Marine Task Force, re-

inforced by a fourth battalion from Saigon, to take the western flank and clear the southwestern wall. The 3d ARVN Regiment would attack south towards the imperial palace, while 1/5 Marines would continue its attack along the southeastern wall. Truong placed his Reconnaissance Company on the right flank of the American battalion so as to keep the battle for the recovery of the imperial palace an all-Vietnamese affair.

From the 18th through the 21st, the Americans and South Vietnamese forces in the Citadel encountered the same dogged resistance that they had throughout the battle. On the 19th, two NVA battalions launched an attack against the 1st Vietnamese Marine Battalion. Although the Vietnamese Marines successfully threw back the attackers with heavy losses, several of the high ranking commanders of the NVA forces in the city used the cover of the assault to make good their escape from the Citadel.

Still, the NVA troops in the city continued to fight

HOUSE SEARCH:
—Marines from the 1st Bn, 5th Marines, approach a house in a sector south of Hue. After the capture of the Citadel, the 1st Battalion joined the 2d Battalion in operations to clear the approaches to Hue.

Taking the tower

IN MEMORIAM:
Mourners gather in 1969 at a mass funeral for the victims of the 1968 "Tet Massacre" in Hue. South Vietnamese authorities attempted to identify all of the dead, checking against the lists of those missing from the city as a result of the fighting.

on, but by the 21st, it was apparent that the end of the struggle for Hue was in sight. To the west, the 1st Cavalry's 3d Brigade overran an enemy regimental command post in the La Chu sector and then extended its perimeter to the Perfume River, closing down the enemy's main supply route. In the Citadel itself, the ARVN forces closed upon the imperial grounds while 1/5 Marines was only one block away from the southeast wall.

The battalion had suffered heavily. In eight days of heavy fighting, 1/5 Marines had sustained over 340 casualties including 47 killed. On the 21st, Company L, 3d Battalion, 5th Marines reinforced

the 1st Battalion for the final push. The following morning the battalion renewed the attack. Slowed by snipers, Company A finally reached the wall at 1300 hours and raised the "National Ensign over the captured objective." According to a Marine report, "Enemy contact was lighter than on any previous day."

To the west, on the same day, ARVN troops and Vietnamese Marines with the assistance of US air support repulsed a last ditch Communist attempt to hold back the inevitable. On the night of 23-24 February, the Vietnamese Marines launched their own surprise attack along the southwestern wall.

At 0500 hours on the 24th, troops of the 3d ARVN Regiment raised the yellow and red flag of the Republic of Vietnam in place of the Viet Cong banner over the fortress wall and finally recaptured the imperial palace. By the next morning, South Vietnamese Marines reduced the last enemy stronghold within the Citadel.

For the US Marines, Operation Hue City lasted about a week longer. The 1/5 Marines joined 2/5 Marines in a two-battalion sweep east and north of the city. Captain Downs of the 2d Battalion recalled that they came across a tremendous tunnel complex extending over 5 miles with overhead cover every 15 meters. As Downs observed, "that had to be a way to get significant reinforcements into the city." Despite uncovering several enemy tunnels and supplies, the Marines encountered few enemy troops. Most of the NVA defenders made good their escape from Hue. As Lieutenant Colonel Cheatham, the commander of the 2d Battalion, noted, "we couldn't close it (the circle around the enemy). To be honest, we didn't have enough people to close it." The Marines ended Operation Hue City on 2 March 1968.

For both sides, the battle had been costly. The allies killed over 5,000 of the Communists and took 89 prisoners. Marine casualties were also high. They suffered 142 killed and over 850 wounded. US Army losses were 74 dead and 507 wounded. The South Vietnamese Army and Marines sustained 384 dead and 1,830 wounded.

The greatest sufferers of the fighting were the city and residents of Hue. More than 50 percent of the city, especially in the Citadel, was reduced to rubble. More than 116,000 people were homeless. Out of a population of about 140,000, some 5,800 were dead or missing.

The smell of death pervaded the city. Once they had captured the city, the Communists had established their own civil government. Communist cadres and special units rounded up groups of people whom they identified as "enemies of the revolution." In the months that followed, the South Vietnamese Government would exhume some 3,000 bodies that were thrown into hasty mass graves. In all probability, these were the victims of the Communist roundups.

In a civilian morgue —Buddhist funeral standards hang over the rough plywood coffins containing bodies dug up by the South Vietnamese after the recapture of Hue. The bodies were thought to be victims of Communist roundups after they captured the city.

VICTIMS:
Villagers line up skulls from newly found mass graves. The graves were found nearly 19 months after the Tet Offensive outside of Hue. In the aftermath of Tet the remains of some 2,800 civilians, killed by the communists, were found in mass graves. Another 3,000 civilians were missing, presumed dead.

As a Vietnamese poet, Trinh Cong Son, wrote:

When I went up a high hill of an afternoon
I sang on top of corpses
I saw, I saw, I saw beside a garden hedge
A mother hugging her child's corpse.

Losing the battle . . .

. . . and winning the war

THE END OF THE BATTLE for Hue signaled the collapse of the enemy Tet Offensive. Both sides began to pick up the pieces and evaluate the situation. According to American estimates, the Communists lost about one-half of their attacking force, nearly 40,000 out of the 84,000 troops committed to the offensive. More significantly, the bulk of these losses were from the irreplaceable local guerrilla forces and VC cadre who made up much of the Communist local infrastructure. US forces sustained casualties of about 4,000, including wounded, and the South Vietnamese suffered about 8,000 men killed. The South Vietnamese pacification program in the countryside was in shreds and more than 800,000 people had become refugees.

In some respects the Offensive had an even larger impact in the United States. Opinion polls showed continuing slippage of public support of administration policy in conducting the war. The American people saw no "light at the end of the tunnel," only a long and difficult war that seemed to have no end.

Concerned about the ability of the United States to meet other commitments, the Chairman of the Joint Chiefs of Staff, General Earle G. Wheeler, maneuvered General Westmoreland to ask for further reinforcements. Wheeler knew full well that such a request would involve the activation of the US Reserves. The bulk of the Reserves would not go to Vietnam, but fill the depleted manpower needs of US forces elsewhere.

This request for additional forces backfired. The newly appointed Secretary of Defense Clark Clifford led the opposition within the Johnson Administration against any further large commitment to

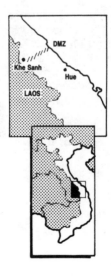

the war. President Johnson approved only a limited reinforcement of troops to Vietnam and no major callup of Reserves.

Many Democrats, who had doubts all along about the course of the war, seized upon the Tet Offensive as an excuse to disassociate themselves from the administration. This dissent began to shape the course of the American Presidential race. In the mid-March New Hampshire Democratic Primary Senator Eugene McCarthy of Minnesota, running on a peace platform, garnered an unexpected 46 percent of the vote against President Johnson—not enough to win, but enough to make a deep impression. At the end of March a disillusioned President surprised the American people by announcing that he would not stand for reelection. At the same time he announced a cutback on the American bombing of North Vietnam.

In many respects, the Tet Offensive was also a setback for the Communist forces in Vietnam. As a captured COSVN document in the Saigon region admitted, the VC failed to seize a number of objectives and "to hold the occupied areas."

The enemy realistically may never have expected his offensive to cause a national uprising throughout South Vietnam. He probably had in mind a more limited and attainable goal. In all likelihood, the Communists used Khe Sanh as a feint in order to mass their forces against Hue. They perhaps hoped that the capture of Hue would result in the defection of the ARVN forces and the loss of other population centers in the two northern provinces. Such a result would have cut the allied lines of communication and left the 3d Marine Division isolated in fixed positions, including Khe Sanh, in the northern border regions along the DMZ and Laos. This would have left the Communists in a strong position for obtaining their own terms.

There is some evidence to support this contention. It was only in northern I Corps that the enemy committed his first-line troops. In the extended battle for Hue City, the 1st Cavalry Division encountered, in mid-February, three North Vietnamese regiments that supposedly were at Khe Sanh. It was also from Hue that the Communists announced the formation of the "New Alliance for National Democratic and Peace Forces" and a new revolutionary government.

Secretary of Defense Clark M. Clifford —Appointed in 1968 after Tet, he steered the Johnson Administration away from any further escalation of the war.

The NVA and Viet Cong were unable to obtain even this limited objective. Although achieving surprise in their capture of Hue, they failed to take two major allied strongholds, the headquarters sector in the Citadel and the MACV compound in southern Hue. From these two toeholds, the allied forces were able to mount their counteroffensive against the enemy troops in the city. The South Vietnamese 1st Division remained loyal to the government and gave a good account of itself. Although Khe Sanh may have been a feint, it caused Westmoreland to shift the 1st Air Cavalry Division north where it was in position to reinforce both Quang Tri City and Hue.

Tet served as a benchmark for both sides. Both the Americans and Vietnamese reassessed their strategies. The United States determined the extent of its commitment to Vietnam and began planning to turn more of the war over to the South Vietnamese Government. American and North Vietnamese negotiators met in Paris in May to discuss the possibility of peace talks. After August 1968, the North Vietnamese and Viet Cong scaled down their large unit war, probably out of both weakness and the expectation that the Americans would eventually withdraw. Tet taught both sides that there was to be no quick fix and victory would lie with whoever decided to stay the course.

Seven years later at 1045 hours local time on 30 April 1975, a Russian-built T-54 tank, the vanguard of the victorious North Vietnamese Army, smashed the gate leading to Independence Palace in Saigon, soon to be renamed Ho Chi Minh City.

AN ELABORATE BLUFF?

A Marine, his face swathed in bandages, walks down a road at Khe Sanh combat base during the 77-day siege. Hindsight suggests that the Communists used Khe Sanh as a feint while they massed their forces for the attack on Hue.

I HAVE USED the following published sources in developing this account of the Tet Offensive:

Peter Braestrup, *The Big Story*, 2 vols. (Boulder, CO: Westview Press, 1972);

Peter Braestrup, editor, *Vietnam as History, Ten Years after the Paris Peace Accords* (Washington: University Press of America, 1984);

Department of Defense, *United States-Vietnam Relations, 1945-1967*, 12 vols. (Washington: Government Printing Office, 1971);

Clark Dougan, Stephen Wise, and the editors of Boston Publishing Company, *Nineteen Sixty-Eight: The Vietnam Experience* (Boston: Boston Publishing Company, 1983);

Vo Nguyen Giap, *Big Victory, Great Task* (New York: Frederick A. Praeger, 1968);

Michael Herr, *Dispatches* (New York: Avon Books, 1978);

Editors, Infantry Magazine, *A Distant Challenge: The US Infantryman in Vietnam, 1967-70* (Birmingham, AL: Birmingham Publishing Company, 1971);

Stanley Karnow, *Vietnam, A History* (New York: The Viking Press, 1983);

Guenter Lewy, *America in Vietnam* (New York: Oxford University Press, 1978);

Col Hoang Ngoc Luong, *The General Offensives of 1968-69: Indochina Monographs* (Washington: US Army Center of Military History, 1981);

Keith B. Nolan, *Battle for Hue, Tet 1968* (Novato, CA: Presidio Press, 1983);

Don Oberdorfer, *Tet!* (New York: Doubleday, 1971);

Dave R. Palmer, *Summons of the Trumpet* (Novato, CA: Presidio Press, 1978);

Lieutenant General Willard Pearson, *The War in the Northern Provinces, 1966-1968, Vietnam Studies* (Washington: Department of the Army, 1975);

Douglas Pike, *War, Peace, and the Viet Cong* (Cambridge, MA: The M.I.T. Press, 1969);

Robert Pisor, *The End of the Line: The Siege of Khe Sanh* (New York: W. W. Norton, 1982);

Herbert Y. Schandler, *The Unmaking of a President: Lyndon Johnson and Vietnam* (Princeton, NJ: Princeton University Press, 1977);

Captain Moyers S. Shore, II, *The Battle for Khe Sanh* (Washington: US Marine Corps, 1969);

Statement of sources

Lieutenant Colonel Pham Van Son and Lieutenant Colonel Le Van Duong, *The Viet Cong Tet Offensive* (Saigon: Joint General Staff, Republic of Vietnam, 1969);

Edwin H. Simmons, *Marines, The Illustrated History of the Vietnam War* (Toronto, London, New York: Bantam Books, 1987);

Shelby L. Stanton, *Vietnam Order of Battle* (Washington: US News Books, 1981);

Shelby L. Stanton, *The Rise and Fall of an American Army, US Ground Forces in Vietnam, 1965-1973* (Novato, CA: Presidio Press, 1985);

William S. Turley, *The Second Indochina War, A Short Political and Military History, 1954-1975*, Mentor edition (New York: New American Library, 1987);

US Marine Corps History and Museums Division, *The Marines in Vietnam, 1954-1975: An Anthology and Annotated Bibliography*, Revised edition (Washington: US Marine Corps, 1986);

War Experiences Recapitulation Committee of the High Level Military Institute, *The Anti-US Resistance War for National Salvation*, (Hanoi: People's Army Publishing House, 1980) (translation in US Foreign Broadcast Information Service, Joint Publications Research Service No. 80968, 3 June 1982);

General William C. Westmoreland, *A Soldier Reports)* (New York: Doubleday, 1976);

General William C. Westmoreland and Admiral U.S.G. Sharp, *Report on the War in Vietnam* (As of 30 June 1968) (Washington: Government Printing Office, 1968).

The author has also made use of documentary and oral history unclassified sources available to the general public located in the Center of Marine Corps History, Washington Navy Yard, Washington, D.C.; US Army Center of Military History, Pulaski Building, Washington, D.C.; Hoover Institution on War, Peace, and Revolution, Stanford University, Stanford, CA; Indochina Archives, Institute of East Asian Studies, University of California, Berkeley, CA.

AK-47	— Russian-designed Kalishnikov gas-operated 7.62mm automatic rifle with an effective range of 400 meters.
Arc Light	— The codename for B-52 bombing missions in South Vietnam.
ARVN	— Army of the Republic of Vietnam (South Vietnam).
B-52	— Boeing Stratofortress, a US Air Force eight-engine, swept-wing, heavy jet bomber.
BLT	— Battalion landing team.
CAP	— See "Combined Action Program."
CH-53	— Sikorsky "Sea Stallion," a single-rotor, heavy transport helicopter powered by two shaft-turbine engines.
CinCPac	— Commander in Chief, Pacific.
CinCPacFlt	— Commander in Chief, Pacific Fleet.
CMC	— Commandant of the Marine Corps.
Combined Action Program	— Marine-initiated pacification technique which integrated a Marine rifle squad with a South Vietnamese Popular Force platoon for hamlet and village security.
Com USMACV	— Commander, US Military Assistance Command, Vietnam.
CP	— Command post, a unit's field headquarters.
CTZ	— Corps Tactical Zone, principal military and political territorial sub-division of the Republic of South Vietnam.
DMZ	— Demilitarized Zone along the 17th Parallel that separated North and South Vietnam. Established by the Geneva Accords of 1954.
F-4B	— McDonnell Phantom II, a twin-engined, two-seat, long-range jet interceptor and attack bomber.
I Corps	— The military and political sub-division which included the five

northern provinces of South Vietnam.

JCS — Joint Chiefs of Staff (United States).

JGS — Joint General Staff (South Vietnam).

KIA — Killed-in-action.

LZ — Landing zone for helicopters.

MAB — Marine Amphibious Brigade.

MACV — Military Assistance Command, Vietnam.

MAF — Marine Amphibious Force.

MAG — Marine Aircraft Group.

Main Force — Organized Viet Cong battalions and regiments as opposed to local VC guerrilla groups or hamlet militia.

NVA — North Vietnamese Army, often used colloquially to refer to a North Vietnamese soldier.

PAVN — Peoples Army of Vietnam (North Vietnam). Usage dropped in favor of "NVA."

PF — Popular Force, South Vietnamese hamlet and village militia.

RF — Regional Force. South Vietnamese provincial militia.

RPG — Rocket propelled grenade.

RVNAF — Republic of Vietnam Armed Forces.

TAOR — Tactical area of operational responsibility.

Tet — Vietnamese for the lunar New Year.

USMC — United States Marine Corps.

VC or Viet Cong — A contraction of the Vietnamese phrase meaning "Vietnamese Communist."

Viet Minh — A contraction of "Viet Nam Doc Lap Nong Minh Hoi," the Communist-led coalition that opposed the French in the First Indo-China War, 1947-1954.

VNAF — Vietnamese Air Force.

WIA — Wounded-in-action.

About
the Author

Jack Shulimson

JACK SHULIMSON is the head of the Histories Section at the Marine Corps Historical Center. He is the author of two of the Marine Corps official volumes on the Vietnam War, has written several articles, and participated in several conferences on the Vietnam War. He has also written extensively on Marine Corps history.

He holds a Bachelor of Arts degree from the University of Buffalo and a Masters Degree in History from the University of Michigan, Ann Arbor. Mr Shulimson has three sons, Mark, Kenneth, and Daniel, and makes his home with his wife Corinne in Bowie, MD.

The Illustrated History of
MARINES
The Vietnam War

EDWIN

The Illustrated History of
ARMOR
The Vietnam War

USMC 211242

The Illustrated History of
KHE SANH
The Vietnam War

The Illustrated History of
SKY SOLDIERS
The Vietnam War

E. CLIFTON BERRY, JR

The Illustrated History of
CARRIER OPERATIONS
The Vietnam War

NF

MICHAEL

EDWARD J. MAROLDA

THE ILLUSTRATED HISTORY OF THE VIETNAM WAR

am's Illustrated History of the
nam War is a unique and new
s of books exploring in depth the
that seared America to the core:
r that cost 58,022 American lives,
saw great heroism and re-
cefulness mixed with terrible
ruction and tragedy.

e Illustrated History of the Viet-
War examines exactly what hap-
d: every significant aspect—the
ical details, the operations and

the strategies behind them—is analyz-
ed in short, crisply written original
books by established historians and
journalists.

Some books are devoted to key battles and campaigns, others unfold the
stories of elite groups and fighting
units, while others focus on the role
of specific weapons and tactics.

Each volume is totally original and
is richly illustrated with photographs,
line drawings, and maps.

AVAILABLE NOW

Sky Soldiers
F. CLIFTON BERRY, JR.
The story of the 173d Airborne, the US combat unit that made the first parachute attack in Vietnam.
$6.95/$8.95 in Canada ISBN:0-553-34320-3

Marines
BRIG. GEN. EDWIN H. SIMMONS
The Marines were the first combat troops into Vietnam and the last to leave. In Vietnam they lived up to their legendary fighting tradition.
$6.95/$8.95 in Canada ISBN:0-553-34448-X

Carrier Operations
EDWARD J. MAROLDA
Yankee and Dixie Stations—two map coordinates in the South China Sea from where the aircraft carriers of the US Seventh Fleet launched for the heaviest bombing campaign in history.
$6.95/$8.95 in Canada ISBN:0-553-34348-3

Armor
JAMES R. ARNOLD
The experts forecast that armor would be useless in Vietnam. But armor was able to move quickly and produce devastating firepower against an enemy constantly on the move.
$6.95/$8.95 in Canada ISBN:0-553-34347-5

Tunnel Warfare
TOM MANGOLD & JOHN PENYCATE
The secret network of tunnels around Saigon was the battleground for the most harrowing campaign of the war as US "Tunnel Rats" took on Viet Cong who had lived for years below ground.
$6.95/$8.95 in Canada ISBN:0-553-34318-1

Khe Sanh
MICHAEL EWING
For 77 days without adequate supplies, 6,000 isolated Marines defended the remote combat base at Khe Sanh.
$6.95/$8.95 in Canada ISBN:0-553-34458-7

Artillery
JAMES R. ARNOLD
Firepower superiority was critical to the US war effort. It led to the fire support bases—a unique development in the use of artillery.
$6.95/$8.95 in Canada ISBN: 0-553-34319-X

Riverine Force
JOHN FORBES & ROBERT WILLIAMS
How the hastily assembled brown water navy overcame the nightmare task of securing South Vietnam's 3,500-mile labyrinth of waterways.
$6.95/$8.95 in Canada ISBN:0-553-34317-3

Strike Aircraft
F. CLIFTON BERRY, JR.
State-of-the-art bombs and missiles revolutionized the art of aerial combat in Vietnam. This is the story of the men, the missions, and the machines.
$6.95/$8.95 in Canada ISBN: 0-553-34508-7

Rangers
JAMES R. ARNOLD
The eerie world of the jungle fighters who probed deep behind enemy lines, snatching prisoners and gathering intelligence.
$6.95/$8.95 in Canada ISBN: 0-553-34509-5

Helicopters
JOHN GUILMARTIN, JR. & MICHAEL O'LEARY
Helicopters revolutionized the war in Vietnam. This is the most comprehensive account so far.
$6.95/$8.95 in Canada ISBN: 0-553-34506-0

Chargers
F. CLIFTON BERRY, JR.
You were either quick or dead in Vietnam. Among the quickest were the 196th Light Infantry—the Chargers. The inside story of a unique unit.
$6.95/$8.95 in Canada ISBN: 0-553-34507-9

Skyraider
Robert F. Dorr
The fascinating story of the A-1 Skyraider, the World War II veteran prop-driven aircraft brought back to fight in a jet-age war.
$6.95/$8.95 in Canada ISBN:0-553-34548-6

Gadget Warfare
F. CLIFTON BERRY, JR.
How faith in the technological fix produced electronic people sniffers, exotic chemical soups that turned trails into mud and gunships that fired 18,000 bullets at a burst.
$6.95/$8.95 in Canada ISBN 0-553-34547-8

Personal Firepower
EDWARD C. EZELL
A compelling and detailed account of the behind-the-scenes arms race that changed the way men on both sides fought.
$6.95/$8.95 in Canada ISBN 0-553-34549-4

Dust Off
JOHN L. COOKE
In Vietnam these MASH-style medevac pilots were a breed apart—brave humanitarians who constantly bent the rules and risked their lives to pluck the wounded from the combat zone.
$6.95/$8.95 in Canada ISBN 0-553-34550-8

Air Cav
F. CLIFTON BERRY, JR.
The story of the trailblazing 1st Air Cavalry and how it pioneered the airmobility concept in Vietnam.
$6.95/$8.95 in Canada ISBN 0-553-34569-9

Available at your local bookstore or call Bantam Books direct at 1-800-223-6834. (In New York State call 212-765-6500 ext. 479.)